I0691721

Samuel W. Curriden

Our Soldiers and Sailors

What they said and did on the tenth anniversary of the battle of Antietam,

at Pittsburg, Penna., September 17th and 18th, 1872

Samuel W. Curriden

Our Soldiers and Sailors
What they said and did on the tenth anniversary of the battle of Antietam, at Pittsburg, Penna., September 17th and 18th, 1872

ISBN/EAN: 9783337307738

Printed in Europe, USA, Canada, Australia, Japan

Cover: Foto ©ninafisch / pixelio.de

More available books at **www.hansebooks.com**

OUR

SOLDIERS AND SAILORS:

WHAT THEY SAID AND DID

ON THE

TENTH ANNIVERSARY OF THE BATTLE OF ANTIETAM,

AT

PITTSBURG, PENNA.,

SEPTEMBER 17TH AND 18TH, 1872.

By SAMUEL W. CURRIDEN,
OFFICIAL STENOGRAPHER.

NEW YORK:
PUBLISHED BY VETERANS' NATIONAL COMMITTEE.
1872.

THE VETERANS' NATIONAL CONVENTION.

THE PRELIMINARY ORGANIZATION.

An informal meeting of soldiers and sailors who were present in Philadelphia, Pa., in attendance upon the Republican National Convention, convened at Assembly Hall, in that city, on the evening of June 5th, and organized with General Ambrose E. Burnside, of Rhode Island, as chairman, and General Daniel Woodall, of Delaware, as secretary. On motion of Col. L. E. Dudley, it was resolved that a committee of one from each State be appointed by the chair, and that said committee be instructed to issue a call for a National Mass Convention of Soldiers and Sailors.

At a meeting held on the following morning the committee was announced, and requested to meet, the same evening, at the Continental Hotel. At the meeting of the committee Gen. A. E. Burnside was added as a member at large, and elected its chairman, and Col. L. E. Dudley was elected secretary. The officers of the committee were then authorized to prepare and issue the call, which they did on the 5th of July, in the following words :—

THE CALL.

HEADQUARTERS VETERANS' NATIONAL COMMITTEE,
FIFTH AVENUE HOTEL,
NEW YORK CITY, July 5, 1872.

To the Soldiers and Sailors who served in the Union Army and Navy during the late War:

Comrades—The undersigned, a committee appointed for the purpose by a meeting of veterans from all sections of the country, who were assembled in Philadelphia upon the 5th day of June, in attendance upon the Republican National Convention, and which meeting unanimously resolved to abide by and support the nominations of said convention, hereby invite you to meet in mass convention at Pittsburg, Pa., on the 17th day of September, 1872, for the purpose of expressing our unreserved belief that the destinies of this country, for the ensuing four years, should be under the protection of men who never faltered in the hour of our country's greatest danger. We believe that men should be placed in high positions of State, who, in the hour of our greatest peril, gave that intellect, personal reputation, and personal faith in the justness of our cause, which was necessary to save the country and place us in the position we now occupy.

We congratulate ourselves upon the fact that the government, during the past three and one-half years, has been administered by one of our comrades, who has shown wonderful civil capacity in aiding the reduction of the public debt, in conducting our foreign affairs with great skill, so that we now stand at peace with the whole world, and in preserving peace in sections of our country where sentiments were entertained calculated to disturb the reorganization of the States lately in rebellion. We have full faith in him as a peaceful man, because, had he felt disposed to exercise his power as a personal governor, he would have done it while nearly a million of men were in arms and under his command, instead of aiding. as he did, the rapid reduction of the army to a peace footing. We believe him to be honest. capable, and courageous.

We believe that it will be a source of pleasure to all who battled for the Union, to meet once more and revive the memories of our old campaigns.

We believe that an expression of the feelings and opinions of those who defended the nation on land and sea would, at this time, be most opportune.

We believe that such an expression would be regarded by all right-thinking men as one proper to be made; and that it would be productive of the most beneficial results.

We believe that our comrades universally desire that such measures shall prevail as will secure the greatest possible happiness and prosperity of the whole people.

We believe that our country's old defenders are actuated by no partisan or factious motives, but are in favor of good government, purity of public men and measures, and the elevation and purification of our institutions.

We believe that while all the old veterans are loyalists in the extreme, and utterly opposed to any doctrine which would tend, in the slightest degree, to revive the heresy of secession, they are desirous of extending charity and full forgiveness to all of their former enemies in the field who now recognize or who may hereafter recognize the great wrong that they have done to our country.

Believing, as we do, that great good will result from the meeting proposed, we most cordially and earnestly invite all our former comrades to meet with us at Pittsburg, on the tenth anniversary of the battle of Antietam, September 17, 1872.

Let us come together again, as we did in 1861, sinking all partisan differences, take our stand now, as then, for our country, and, before and beyond all else, labor for her honor and glory.

Fraternally yours,
GENERAL A. E. BURNSIDE, Chairman.

L. E. DUDLEY, *Secretary.*

Gen. POWELL CLAYTON,	Gen. J. T. AVERILL,	Capt. BARBOUR LEWIS,
" GEORGE E. SPENCER,	Maj. O. C. FRENCH,	Gen. W. G. VEASEY,
Col. JAMES COEY,	B. B. CAHOON,	Capt. W. H. H. STOWELL,
Gen. R. J. OGELSBY.	Gen. A. M. DENNISON,	Col. JAMES H. PLATT,
" SOL. D. MEREDITH,	" A. F. STEVENS,	Gen. LUCIUS FAIRCHILD,
" GRENVILLE M. DODGE,	" WILLIAM WARD,	Col. JAMES LEWIS,
Lieut. Col. R. J. HINTON,	" S. L. WOODFORD,	Gen. JOSEPH C. ABBOTT,
Gen. JOHN M. HARLAN,	" F. C. BARLOW,	" E. F. NOYES,
" JAS. D. FESSENDEN,	" DANIEL WOODALL,	" JAMES S. NEGLEY,
" SELDEN CONNER,	" CHAS. M. HAMILTON,	" EDWARD McCOOK,
" HORACE B. SARGEANT.	" LOUIS C. WAGNER,	" N. P. CHIPMAN.
" J. H. DUVALL,	" C. H. T. COLLIS,	Maj. JOSEPH W. HOUSTON,
" E. W. HINKS.	" A. L. PIERSON,	Gen. B. F. POTTS,
" JOSEPH R. HAWLEY,	Capt. A. W. NORRIS,	Col. WILLIAM BREEDEN,
" JAS. H. VAN ALEN,	Gen. CHARLES R. BRAYTON,	Gen. GEO. A. MAXWELL,
" F. W. SWIFT.	" JAMES DAVIDSON,	" J. W. FISHER.

All soldiers and sailors who approve the objects of this call, are requested to communicate with the committee, at the Fifth Avenue Hotel, New York City.

• Immediately after promulgating the call, the committee prepared blanks and distributed them throughout the country, with a view of securing an expression of the veterans upon the views set forth in the call, and received the signatures of fully fifty thousand soldiers and sailors, in approval of the objects of the Convention.

While the committee believed that the Convention itself would be of great service in the campaign, it decided that, if thorough organization of the veterans of the country could be secured, that much effective work could be done and that the results of the Convention would be felt in every State; therefore the following circular letter was sent to prominent veterans in each State, and in most has resulted in the formation of veterans' clubs, to act in harmony with and aid the regular Republican organizations.

LETTER INVITING ORGANIZATION.

HEADQUARTERS VETERANS' NATIONAL COMMITTEE,
FIFTH AVENUE HOTEL,
NEW YORK CITY, July 30, 1872.

Dear Sir—I take great pleasure in informing you that the call of this committee for a National Convention of Veterans at Pittsburg, Pa., Sept. 17th, has met with a most hearty response from individual veterans of all ranks from every State. No doubt now exists that our reunion will eclipse all former ones in point of numbers, enthusiasm, and importance. We feel confident that not less than twenty-five thousand veterans will be in attendance. Many clubs and associations will attend *en masse*.

It is believed that this meeting, if preceded and followed by thorough organization of the old soldiers in every town and city throughout the Union, would be one of the most potential agencies that could be brought to bear in this campaign. It would arouse, among all classes of citizens, the old feeling of patriotism and devotion to the country which was its salvation in the time of war.

We desire to institute such organizations *at once* in every State, and desire to enlist your active co-operation. Will you endeavor to organize the veterans of your State, or induce some one, or more, in whom you have confidence, to immediately inaugurate such a movement? If you could correspond with prominent veterans in every county, and suggest to them the propriety of organizing a "Grant and Wilson Veterans' Association" in every town in their respective counties, each of these clubs could send as large a delegation as possible to Pittsburg, and thereby swell the gathering and increase the enthusiasm there, and, returning from thence, they would permeate the whole country with the old feeling of patriotism and devoted loyalty.

This committee cordially invite correspondence from all local organizations, and will take pleasure in affording all information in their power.

Please reply at your earliest convenience, that we may know what to expect from your State.

Very truly yours,
A. E. BURNSIDE,
Chairman.

L. E. DUDLEY, *Secretary.*

LETTERS RECEIVED.

In response to the call several thousand letters were received from all sections of the country. To give all these letters in full would take much more space than can be afforded in these pages; but we have selected a few of the more important, with extracts from many others.

FROM GENERAL O. O. HOWARD.

ASTOR HOUSE, NEW YORK CITY, July 15, 1872.

GEN. A. E. BURNSIDE, *Chairman Veterans' National Committee, Fifth Avenue Hotel, New York City:*

Dear General—Your circular, accompanied by the kind invitation of your secretary to be present on the anniversary of the battle of Antietam, and take part in the exercises at Pittsburg, 17th of September next, is just received. I have carefully read your call, and am willing to adopt its sentiments as my own. I am, perhaps, for a very warm recognition of those who have been our enemies, when they step upon our platform, and would most heartily say, "Let us be brethren." I believe it is better, more for the durability of our Government, and certainly safer to our public credit, that no radical change of administration should now take place. I am very much interested in the Indian tribes that are now rapidly coming into the light of our civilization. I should dislike exceedingly to have the great body of religious and benevolent societies suddenly deprived of the privilege of nominating agencies, which has begun to work so grandly in the line of reform; and for a thousand other reasons, besides my personal feelings of sincere regard for him who has led us to victory and to safety, my words and my acts will be in behalf of the present incumbent of the presidential chair. I am an army officer, without partisan feeling, ready to do my duty under any leader my countrymen shall select; but, God knows that I do love a man like Gen. Grant, who does persevere in words and in acts in the practical recognition of human rights to all classes of our fellow-men. I fear that I will not be able to join you at Pittsburg, as my duties are likely to keep me on the frontier.

Sincerely yours,
O. O. HOWARD.

FROM GENERAL B. S. ROBERTS.

NEW HAVEN, July 11, 1872.

L. E. DUDLEY, *Secretary :*

Dear Sir—Your circular and note came to me this morning, although dated 8th instant. Instead of putting forth any opinion I may have of Gen. Grant, as it could not possibly have influence with parties, partisans, or politicians, I send you an autograph letter of the late Major Gen. George H. Thomas, that goes directly to the great issues of the day, and is an expression of the judgment of the soundest and most solid soldier of the Union Army, who knew Gen. Grant intimately and thoroughly.

Were Gen. Thomas living, I do not doubt—modest and silent as he was by nature, and by education and habit averse to notoriety and meaningless public applause—that his pen and voice would have sustained Grant now, as his sword and loyal nature sustained him when he smote Hood "hip and thigh" at Nashville, and destroyed the last hope of the rebellion. I consider the meeting of the veterans at Pittsburg as the flank movement of the campaign, that, more than any other single evolution, is to decide the election. It is my purpose to attend in person, and to use my influence in gathering others from New England at Pittsburg. When the old veterans sound their "assembly" it is a terrible "bugle-blast" for the enemy, and certainly none know so well as they where the enemy's magazines are, and how to drop bombs and shells to explode them.

Very truly yours,
B. S. ROBERTS,
Brigadier-General United States Army (retired).

WHAT GENERAL GEORGE H. THOMAS THOUGHT.

The following is the letter from Gen. Thomas, referred to above:—

SAN FRANCISCO, CAL., Dec. 8, 1869.

GEN. B. S. ROBERTS:

Dear General—I have had your letter of the 22d of November in my possession some days, but have not had leisure to reply until to-day. Many persons have of late spoken to me of the probabilities of the next four years. I have invariably declined all propositions affecting myself, and I now again do so to you. I do not approve of the railroad speed with which the people of the United States do things. We have no stability, but are constantly not only on the go, but rush matters to the verge of confusion, if not of ruin. I sometimes think we, as a people, are specially guarded by an all-wise Providence, else our recklessness would have long since involved the nation in hopeless confusion. No sooner are public affairs rescued from discord, and the offices filled with men who to all appearances are the undoubted choice of the people, than new combinations are formed to destroy the incumbents—if not in character, at least in usefulness—and set up a new set almost unknown, and certainly of doubtful experience. I would not like to see any alteration in the executive for the next eight years, unless the present incumbent should prove incapacitated for his position before the expiration of his first term. I think he has commenced very fair, and I sincerely hope he may succeed to such a degree as to compel his re-election for another term.

I am very truly yours,
GEORGE H. THOMAS.

FROM GOV. NOYES.

COLUMBUS, OHIO, July 16, 1872.

GEN. A. E. BURNSIDE, *Chairman Veterans' National Committee, Fifth Avenue Hotel, New York City :*

General—I have the honor to acknowledge receipt of your favor of the 8th instant. I shall take great satisfaction in co-operating with your committee to the end that the Pittsburg

Convention. Sept. 17th, may be a success. I shall send circulars all over the State in a few days, and will soon forward to you the names and addresses of prominent soldiers and sailors, in order that you may communicate with them from headquarters directly. In my judgment the importance of this meeting cannot be overrated. I shall see you at the convention.

Very truly your obedient servant,

EDWARD F. NOYES.

FROM GENERAL E. W. RICE.

WASHINGTON, D. C., July 8, 1872.

GEN. A. E. BURNSIDE, *Chairman Veterans' National Committee, Fifth Avenue Hotel, New York City :*

General—I beg to assure you of my most hearty approval of the call for a general convention of soldiers and sailors of the late war, to meet at Pittsburg on the 17th of September next.

When Gen. Grant was first nominated, the voice of the soldiers and sailors was unanimously and enthusiastically expressed at our convention at Chicago, and was gloriously seconded by the delegates of the loyal masses in the Republican Convention the following day, notwithstanding the well-known fact that many Republican politicians were opposed to the soldiers' choice. Now, the great voting masses of the Republican party, appreciating the integrity and wisdom of the administration, have, through their instructed delegates at Philadelphia, again tendered us our chief as a candidate for the presidency, and again he is bitterly assailed and violently opposed by the politicians who did not succeed in dictating his policy or controlling his patronage; and it is not only proper, but exceedingly important that we assemble and respond to their announced confidence and desire in terms as honest and earnest as they expressed them, and give them the positive assurance of our hearty indorsement of their action, and make known our great anxiety that the Government shall continue in its present policy, and under control of its friends who preserved its integrity and its honor, and that it may be shielded from those who seek to seize it for purely personal purposes and divide its favors and its revenue with its enemies. I will be with you at Pittsburg, and have the honor to be, General, Very respectfully your obedient servant,

E. W. RICE,
Late Brevet Major-General from Iowa.

FROM COLONEL T. W. HIGGINSON.

NEWPORT, R. I., August 8, 1872.

L. E. DUDLEY, ESQ., *Secretary Veterans' National Committee :*

Dear Sir—Thank you for your invitation to be present at the Pittsburg Convention and to address it. I shall do so, if possible, and, at any rate, the Convention will have my best wishes.

I wish frankly to say that I was opposed to the renomination of President Grant, but am in favor of his election. I see no reason for deserting to the enemy because I have exercised the soldier's privilege of grumbling at my general.

There seems to me no safety for the reconstruction measures except in the hands of the party which passed them.

The main war-cry of the new party appears to be the overthrow of centralization; and what they call centralization is simply the effort of a national government to save itself from being murdered. In such a contest, I am with the Government.

Very truly yours,
THOMAS WENTWORTH HIGGINSON,
Late Colonel Thirty-third U. S. C. T.

FROM GENERAL CHARLES DEVENS, JR.

WORCESTER, MASS., July 18, 1872.

Dear Sir—I have your note on behalf of the committee, requesting me to be present at the Convention in Pittsburg, on the 17th of September, and am much honored by it. My engagements render it absolutely impossible for me to accept it, but I sincerely trust that the gathering will prove of great advantage to the good cause.

Yours very respectfully,
CHAS. DEVENS, JR.

To L. E. DUDLEY, *Sec'y Vets. Nat. Com.*

FROM GENERAL JAMES S. NEGLEY.

"I am warmly interested in the movement contemplated by the National Committee of Veterans. The proposed Convention at Pittsburg, on Sept. 17th, has induced me to change my intention of visiting the Pacific coast this summer. I shall remain at home to contribute personal attention to the objects of the assembly. Six years since (1866) I enjoyed the satisfaction of witnessing an immense gathering of returned soldiers in Pittsburg. The enthusiasm produced in the State by the meeting yielded profitable results at the October election of that year."

FROM GENERAL M. D. LEGGETT.

WASHINGTON, D. C., July 16, 1872.

Dear Sir—I have just returned from a trip West, and find your favor inviting me to attend and address a meeting at Pittsburg, of the old army and navy, in September. If alive, I shall certainly give myself the pleasure of attending that meeting, and if occasion offers, will speak as the spirit may move. My head and heart are in full accord with the object of that meeting.

Very respectfully,

Col. L. E. DUDLEY, *Sec'y, etc.*   M. D. LEGGETT.

FROM GENERAL M. F. FORCE.

CINCINNATI, August 16, 1872.

Col. L. E. DUDLEY, *Secretary :*

Colonel—Your letter inviting me to the Convention of Soldiers and Sailors, to be held at Pittsburg next month, came while I was out of town. I am glad such a convention is to be held. We, who knew General Grant in the field, when the stress of emergencies brought the inmost traits of character to the surface, know he is an honest, sober, pure-minded man, upright, faithful, patient, devoted to duty, and those who know him best honor him most.

As persons holding the office of judge abstain from taking part in political meetings, I refrain from going to this, but I cannot refrain from having and expressing an opinion about our old leader.

Four years ago, while whisky was selling all over the country for less than the tax on its production, distillers and tax-gatherers were growing rich; now the "Whisky Ring" has passed away, and officials do their strict duty. Four years ago the combination called the "Indian Ring" was so strongly intrenched that it was held impregnable. It has vanished, and supplies for the Indians are purchased and disbursed honestly. Four years ago our difficulties with England seemed inextricable, and many people looked for war for a settlement. England has made apology in a solemn treaty, and all questions are disposed of in a way honorable to both nations.

Long usage, amounting to an unwritten amendment to the Constitution, has thrown into the hands of the members of Congress the substantial appointment of a large part of the public offices, and these appointments being naturally given for political service, some bad appointments are inevitable. Gen. Grant, almost unaided and alone, has attempted to cut this evil up by the roots. His aim is shown in the appointments left in the actual control of the President: the Indian Commissioners, the Commissioners to treat with England, and the Geneva appointments, are above cavil.

His treatment of the Southern people has been, from Lee's surrender to the present day, just without harshness, kind and magnanimous without sentimentality.

Comparing his administration not with an ideal standard, but with the condition of things four years ago, it is fair to say that he has done at least as much as any other President to improve and elevate the public service. The cloud of abuse which disappointed men have blown about him will, in due time, pass away, and his administration will shine in history.

Very respectfully yours,

M. F. FORCE.

FROM GENERAL JAMES A. EKIN.

LOUISVILLE, KY., August 2, 1872.

Col. L. E. DUDLEY, *Secretary Veterans' National Committee, Fifth Avenue Hotel, N. Y. City :*

My Dear Colonel—I have the honor to acknowledge the receipt of your letter of the 16th ult., informing me that "A Grand National Mass Convention of Veterans will be held at

Pittsburg, Penn., on the tenth anniversary of the battle of Antietam, the 17th of September next," and inviting me to be present and address the Convention.

Absence from the city has prevented an earlier reply.

Pittsburg is my native city, and to meet my brother veterans at my old home, in the midst of my friends and neighbors, on such an interesting and important occasion, will afford me unspeakable pleasure.

Your kind invitation is most heartily accepted, and I trust that nothing may prevent me from being with you at the time indicated.

I sympathize fully with the object of the contemplated Convention, and it affords me unfeigned pleasure to indorse the sentiments of the committee, "that the destinies of this country for the ensuing four years should be under the protection of men who never faltered in the hour of our country's greatest danger."

I sincerely believe that this sentiment will receive a hearty response from the true and noble men throughout the Republic, and will be ratified by the American people in a manner that will gladden the hearts of not only the men who periled their lives in defense of the flag, but of all those who love and desire the perpetuation of the liberties we now enjoy. May they be perpetual. Heartily thanking you for your invitation, and with my best wishes for the triumph of the principles represented by your patriotic organization,

I am, dear sir, very respectfully,
JAMES A. EKIN,
Brevet. Brig.-Genl. U. S. A.

FROM GENERAL SELDEN CONNOR.

AUGUSTA, MAINE, July 27, 1872.

Col. L. E. DUDLEY, *Secretary Veterans' National Committee :*

Dear Sir—I regret exceedingly that I am unable to accept the invitation you extend to me to address the Mass Convention of Soldiers and Sailors which is to be held at Pittsburg on the 17th of September next.

I can well believe that the defenders of the Union, gathered together in such an assemblage to do it peaceful service, reviewing the glorious results accomplished by their great chief in leading the country through peace to prosperity, regarding the patriotic and consistent course of the party of the Union, and confronting the thinly disguised dangers that threaten the country in the efforts of a selfish opposition to obtain power, will be re-animated by the enthusiasm of devotion to country that inspired them in '61.

The citizen-soldiers, who aided in the preservation of the Union, have watched with deep interest and approval the process of its restoration to perfect integrity, and rejoice at the result.

They have also viewed with satisfaction the careful regard of the government for the national credit and honor.

The treaty with England especially calls forth their hearty commendation. With the memories of slain comrades and of all the cruel scenes of war still fresh in their minds, and filling them with loathing of the barbarity of the resort to arms, they regard with earnest thankfulness the patient perseverance by which the Soldier-President has accomplished the peaceful and honorable settlement of a question that was dark with threatenings of war.

They feel that the denial by his opponents of credit to the executive head of the Government, for the beneficent measures which he has recommended and carried into effect, is as unjust as would be the withholding from Grant of the credit for the victory that came to our arms under his leadership.

Truth, honor, consistency, and patriotism, imperatively call upon the defenders of the Union to stand by their colors and support the party whose record is one of the benefits to the country.

Fraternally yours,
SELDEN CONNOR.

FROM GENERAL J. B. KIDDOO.

PARIS, FRANCE, September 2, 1872.

L. E. DUDLEY, *Secretary, etc. :*

My Dear Sir—Your kind letter of July 16, inviting me to be present and address the Convention of Veterans to be held at Pittsburg on the 17th inst., has just been received. I regret to state that my present plans will not permit me to return to the United States in time to participate in your deliberations.

Though it is not customary for officers of the army to take an active part in politics, I do not hesitate, in consideration of the peculiar nature of the present campaign and its relation to our late war, to express my earnest preference for the re-election of Gen. Grant, and am at a loss to know how any soldier who took an honorable part in the struggle for the maintenance of the Government can possibly take any other view of existing affairs. It would be a sad comment on the achievements of our arms, and a virtual loss of the moral of our victories, if, in less than eight years after the close of the war, the leaders in the Southern rebellion and their Northern allies should be restored to the control of the affairs of the nation.

The soldiers and sailors who fought for the life of the nation should not forget that the party which now opposes the re-election of Gen. Grant includes within its ranks *all* who during the war thought we were the aggressors on civil liberty and the violators of the Constitution, in our efforts to maintain the integrity of the Union by force of arms.

The country owes General Grant a second term, not more for his great achievements during the war than for the success of his administration, which, though it may be exceptionable in some respects, is as free from serious mistakes as any administration since that of Washington.

With the assurance that you will have a reception due heroes in the loyal city of Pittsburg, in which I lived most of my life, and from which I entered the army at the beginning of the war, and with many regrets that I cannot be present,

I remain your obedient servant,
J. B. KIDDOO,
Brigadier-General U. S. A. (retired list.)

FROM GENERAL JOHN M. THAYER.

LINCOLN, NEB., September 12, 1872.

COL. L. E. DUDLEY, *Secretary Veterans' National Committee:*

I had fully intended to meet with the veterans at Pittsburg, on the 17th and 18th insts., but my engagements for speaking in this State prevent. I am, therefore, most reluctantly compelled to forego the pleasure of being present.

But it is a satisfaction to believe that the same high sense of patriotic duty, which moved the hearts of the true soldiers in the late war, will govern those who meet with you now.

We followed our great leader, Grant, then; so let us march under his banner now.

Very truly yours,
JOHN M. THAYER.

FROM PRIVATE TANNER, WHO LOST BOTH LEGS IN BATTLE.

BROOKLYN, N. Y., August 12, 1872.

COL. L. E. DUDLEY, *Secretary Veterans' National Committee:*

Dear Sir—Yours of recent date, inclosing call for Convention at Pittsburg, and inviting myself to attend, is at hand.

In response, I beg leave to say that every pulsation of my heart beats in unison with the proposed objects of said convention, and I shall consider it a high honor to attend, and by voice and vote to participate in its action.

Judging the feelings of other veterans by my own, I presume no class of our citizens are really more in favor of truly and speedily healing over " the bloody chasm" which now separates the two great sections of our country; but we have learned too thoroughly what that chasm involves to indulge in any glittering generalities concerning it, and earnestly desire to rebuild upon a sound basis.

If we evince a disposition to reject in the structure any of the Democratic Ku-Klux bricks, it is because we so fully realize that they are not of standard durability.

Because I distrust the sincerity of Mr. Greeley's sudden abrogation of all party obligations; because I distrust the sincerity of his present supporters, most of whom have been his life-long opponents; but, mostly because of my unlimited faith in the patriotic unselfishness, unlimited devotion to duty, principle, and the best interests of the country, of Ulysses S. Grant and Henry Wilson, am I determined to stand unwavering and zealously for the nominees of the Philadelphia Convention, the truest exponents of American nationality and of the party of Liberty, Progress, and Reform.

Very respectfully yours,
JAMES TANNER,
Late Private 87th N. Y. Vols.

FROM GEN. BEN. SPOONER.

INDIANAPOLIS, August 8, 1872.

L. E. DUDLEY, ESQ., *Secretary Veterans' National Committee, New York City:*

Dear Sir—I am in receipt of your favor of the 1st inst., inviting me to be present and address the Convention of Veterans to be held at Pittsburg on the 17th Sept. I have read the call, and most heartily concur in the purposes for which the convention is to be convened. The political canvass now pending before the people of this country devolves, in my judgment, a duty upon the soldiers and sailors of the late Union army, equal in importance to the safety of the Union and the preservation of the rights of the people, to the great duty so gallantly discharged by them in defending the nation against the greatest rebellion known in the world's history. Secession and rebellion were inaugurated under the auspices of the Democratic party; and for the hundreds of thousands of lives sacrificed in defense of the flag —for the untold and immeasurable suffering entailed upon the people—for the widows' tears and the orphans' cries, and for the mountain of debt which rested so heavily upon the country at the close of the war, the leaders of this party should be held responsible. The election of Mr. Greeley means the elevation of the Democratic party to power, and the elevation of that party to power means the payment of pensions to rebel soldiers as pensions are paid to Union soldiers—means payment for the emancipated slaves at an estimated value of two thousand million dollars—means a recognition of the doctrine that a State has a right to secede from the Union at her pleasure, and means the restoration of the lost cause.

When the poodle-dog succeeds in swallowing and merging into himself the elephant, it will be time enough to consider the silly propositions that a few thousand Liberal Republicans can swallow up and merge into themselves a great party of three millions of voters. It is simply a *trick* to put the Democratic party into power, and it seems to me that every Union soldier and sailor should use his best efforts to defeat the monstrous conspiracy. I gave an entire arm in battling against Mr. Greeley's heresy of secession, as advocated so earnestly by him in the latter part of 1860 and the early part of 1861, and I am not willing now to aid in his elevation to the Presidency, where he can have an opportunity to press his secession views into practical operations. If the people want peace, want quiet and rest—if they want stability and prosperity in the business and financial concerns of the country—if they want economy in the management of public affairs—if they want to transmit to the keeping of their children the best and strongest government on earth, they should stand by the Republican party, and earnestly support Grant and Wilson for President and Vice-President. I hope to attend the convention, but cannot promise to make a speech. May this meeting of my comrades be, in every regard, a great success. Remember me kindly to Gen. Burnside.

Very truly,
BEN. SPOONER.

FROM GENERAL THOMAS C. FLETCHER.

ST. LOUIS, August 5, 1872.

L. E. DUDLEY, *Secretary Veterans' National Committee:*

Dear Sir—In response to the cordial invitation of the committee, tendered me through you, I have to say, that unless prevented by demands upon my time by the Republican party of this State, I will certainly be present and address the mass Convention of Veterans at Pittsburgh, Pa., on the 17th proximo.

In the earnest hope and candid expectation of the election of Grant and Wilson,

I am, truly yours,
THOS. C. FLETCHER.

FROM GENERAL A. HICKENLOOPER.

CINCINNATI, August 6, 1872.

L. E. DUDLEY, ESQ., *Secretary, Fifth Avenue Hotel, New York:*

Sir—I have the honor to acknowledge the receipt of your kind invitation to be present at, and address the meeting of veterans of late war, to be held at Pittsburg, Pa., Sept. 17th. While I fully sympathize with the objects of the meeting, my business engagements are such that it will be impossible for me to attend.

Respectfully,
A. HICKENLOOPER.

FROM GENERAL WALTER HARRIMAN.

CONCORD, N. H., September 15, 1872.

Dear General—It is a source of painful regret that I am compelled to forego the pleasure of attending the Soldiers' and Sailors' Convention on the 17th instant.

I delivered an address in Canterbury yesterday—Saturday—and in coming home by carriage after meeting took a severe cold, so that to-day I am unable to leave my room. I intended to start to-morrow morning—had made all my arrangements to do so—was animated with the expectation of serving in this Pittsburgh campaign under my old and honored commander, and I know not how to reconcile myself to this defeat of my long-contemplated plans.

If possible, without risk to my life, I shall start to-morrow morning, and so reach Pittsburg Tuesday afternoon, but at this moment the prospect is almost hopeless.

Hoping you will have a most successful convention, I subscribe myself,

Yours, with great regard,

WALTER HARRIMAN.

Major-General A. E. BURNSIDE.

FROM GENERAL MICHAEL KERWIN.

NEW YORK, August 3, 1872.

COL. L. E. DUDLEY, *Secretary Veterans' National Committee:*

Dear Sir—Your favor of the 1st instant, inviting me to be present and address the Veterans' Convention to be held at Pittsburg, Pa., September 17th, is at hand.

Permit me, in reply, to thank you for the invitation, and to assure you of my hearty and earnest support. I would at any time deem it a high honor, as well as a pleasure, to meet in convention so many of my old comrades in arms; but to be present on the coming occasion I regard as a duty—an imperative duty, that every loyal Union soldier owes to the country, for the preservation of which he fought and suffered so many privations.

It is high time that loyal men should awake to the new dangers that threaten the nation. The friends of secession are again mustering their forces, and we should show by our action at Pittsburg that we are unwilling to permit the institutions, preserved at so fearful a cost, to fall into the hands of those who sought to destroy them. It is no longer a question of Republicanism and Democracy, two great parties struggling for power, both aiming to promote the interests of the Union. All the old landmarks of the Democratic party are completely obliterated, and its broken fragments are now marshaling under the leadership of the great champion of the doctrine of secession, who, during the dark days of rebellion and treason, tried to embarrass the Government and discourage the friends of the Union by his clamoring for peaceful dissolution. I am happy to be able to assure you, from my numerous acquaintance among the old veterans of the war, that, regardless of all past political connection, the determination is to unite once more under the glorious old flag, and march to the front in defense of the Union and equal rights to all men.

I have the honor to be, very truly,

M. KERWIN,

Late Col. 13th Penna. Cavalry and Brev. Brig.-Gen'l. Vols.

FROM GENERAL WILLIAM VANDEVER.

DUBUQUE, IOWA, August 16, 1872.

COL. L. E. DUDLEY, *Secretary Veterans' National Committee:*

Dear Sir—Your favor of July 16th, inviting me to be present and address the Convention of Veterans at Pittsburg, on the 17th of September, came during my absence from home. I now hasten to reply. It is impossible for me to determine at this time whether I can be present or not; but, whether present or absent, my heart is in sympathy with the object of this meeting. I cannot, for the life of me, see how any citizen who values the Union and desires its preservation, can vote to elevate to the presidency of the States the man who has deliberately avowed that, "whenever assured the Southern people desire separation, he will joyfully co-operate with them to secure the end they seek." The election of such a man would invite disunion. The heroic achievements of the Union army are valueless, if such a philosophy is now to prevail, and we had better abandon the ceremony of decorating with flowers the graves of our dead comrades, as an idle mockery, if the chief advocate of such a sentiment is to be elected President.

The firmness, moderation, and wisdom of the present Chief Magistrate of the Republic, displayed in the field and in council, entitle him to the continued confidence of the people, and are a certain guaranty that he will wisely administer the government another four years.

With great respect, your obedient servant,

WILLIAM VANDEVER.

FROM GENERAL A. T. A. TORBETT.

MILFORD, DELAWARE, August 29, 1872.

To Col. L. EDWIN DUDLEY, *Secretary of Veterans' National Committee :*

Dear Sir—It gives me great pleasure to inform you that it is my desire and intention to be present at the Soldiers' Convention, to be held at Pittsburg on the 17th of September next, there to join with my former associates in any measures which will promote the success of the grand National Republican party in the present contest.

Very respectfully,

A. T. A. TORBETT.

FROM GENERAL C. E. LIPPINCOTT.

SPRINGFIELD, ILLINOIS, August 3, 1872.

Gen. L. E. DUDLEY, *Secretary of Veterans' National Committee :*

Dear Sir—It is the result of accident only that your favor of July 16th has been so long unanswered. I will now say that I was greatly pleased at this movement, and will do all in my power to induce others to attend. I shall attend, unless something now unforeseen shall prevent. Do not count on me for a speech.

Very respectfully, your obedient servant,

C. E. LIPPINCOTT.

FROM GENERAL J. A. WILLIAMSON.

DES MOINES, IOWA, July 31, 1872.

L. E. DUDLEY, *Secretary of Veterans' National Committee, New York :*

Sir—Your favor of the 26th inst., inclosing call for the Soldiers' and Sailors' Convention, is at hand.

In reply to the invitation of the committee to be present and address the Convention at Pittsburg, on the 17th of September, I have to say that I shall take great pleasure in doing so.

I am very respectfully, your obedient servant,

J. A. WILLIAMSON.

FROM GENERAL GEORGE H. PATRICK.

MONTGOMERY, ALABAMA, September 11, 1872.

Col. L. E. DUDLEY, *Sec'y of Veterans' National Committee, Fifth Avenue Hotel, New York City :*

Dear Sir—Inclosed find duplicate credentials of Alabama delegation to National Convention at Pittsburg on 17th inst., the original being sent at hands of Captain R. M. Reynolds, State Auditor, with our greeting that the soldiers of Alabama, with one single and noticeable exception, will vote solid next November for their old commander; and trusting that every State will do as well, I remain

Yours, truly,

GEORGE H. PATRICK.

FROM GENERAL E. F. WINSLOW.

ST. LOUIS, MO., August 6, 1872.

Col. L. E. DUDLEY, *Sec'y of Veterans' National Committee, Fifth Avenue Hotel, New York :*

Dear Sir—In response to the invitation to be present at a mass convention to be held at Pittsburg, September 17th next, I take great pleasure in saying it will afford me sincere gratification to meet my old comrades at that time and place, and that we can cordially unite in the support of our great commander during the present campaign, in which he is certain to lead, as usual, to victory.

I cannot conceive a good reason why one of us can abandon our colors, our leader, or our principles so much as to remain passive during the present contest, and it is much more difficult to believe in a *change of front* and its consequences to the side of union and victory.

When the issues are more clearly defined and the consequences contingent upon a possible failure more fully understood, I am confident the men who stood shoulder to shoulder so firmly will again close up their ranks and move forward as a part of the great civilizing and progressive republican column, to a success as great as that of the last presidential campaign. This civil and political fight will be no less important to the future of our great, united, and now pacified and prosperous country, than was that last named. We all interpreted our situation at that time clearly and intelligently, and I have faith to believe we will see, as distinctly as then, our whole duty at this critical juncture. Certainly our recently enfranchised citizens are not more likely than we to learn what is best for *them*, and as they have already, in one great canvas, fixed their position, we would be less entitled to our claim of superiority if we failed to know our duty or to do it.

Yours fraternally,
E. F. WINSLOW.

FROM GENERAL DENNIS F. BURKE.

NEW YORK, August 1, 1872.

Col. L. E. DUDLEY, *Secretary Veterans' National Committee:*

Dear Colonel—Your letter of the 1st inst., inviting me to be present at the National Convention of Veterans, to be held at Pittsburg, Pa., September 17th, is at hand.

I cordially accept your invitation, and look forward to the time with pleasure, and have an earnest desire to meet many of my former comrades of the army. The old Irish Brigade followed the fortunes of the Army of the Potomac from the beginning of the war to the end. The bones of four-fifths of its members, who fell in the struggle to preserve a united country, lie mingled with the soil of Virginia and Maryland. Many of its members still survive to relate their victories and the hardships they endured. They have returned to their homes, and take a deep interest in the prosperity and welfare of their adopted country. As they stood beneath the folds of our glorious national flag in time of war, battling for freedom to all men, so do they now desire to stand ready to maintain in peace what they sacrificed so much for in time of war.

Confident that we have truth and justice on our side, and that it will prevail, and feeling proud of having served under General Grant, and proud to have the privilege of voting for him, I am, with much respect and high regards,

Yours,
D. F. BURKE,
Brevet Brigadier-General U. S. A. (late Irish Brigade).

FROM GENERAL WILLIAM S. HILLYER.

NEW YORK, August 29, 1872.

My Dear Colonel—Your kind invitation, made on behalf of the Veterans' National Committee, to be present and address the Mass Convention of Soldiers and Sailors of the late war, at Pittsburg on the 17th of September next, was received at my office during my temporary absence from the city.

I take the earliest opportunity to accept the invitation and express to you my cordial sympathy and co-operation in the movement. I will meet you at Pittsburg and do whatever I can to aid in the indorsement of the man who was first in war, and is now first in peace and first in the hearts of his countrymen.

Very respectfully yours, etc.,
WILLIAM S. HILLYER.

Col. L. E. DUDLEY, *Secretary, etc.*

FROM CAPTAIN JAMES H. WITHINGTON.

SAN FRANCISCO, CAL., August 31, 1872.

Col. L. E. DUDLEY, *Secretary Veterans' National Executive Committee:*

Dear Sir—As I am chairman of the Veterans' Executive Committee of this State, I take the liberty of addressing you upon the political outlook in this section.

The soldiers and sailors of the late war are organizing throughout the State, and it is their intention to take a prominent part in the coming campaign. Our organization here is larger than four years ago, and, I am proud to say, has the respect and confidence of this community. It is our intention to so amend our constitution as to admit to membership the veterans of the Mexican war, there being quite a number of this gallant band in our midst.

Also those Confederate soldiers who have more confidence in Grant, the general who made peace, than Greeley, the editor who wrote up the war.

There are a large number of the above-mentioned soldiers awaiting an opportunity to join us. There are about as many old Confederate soldiers here as there are Union soldiers.

We are peculiarly situated in this respect. We propose "to bridge the bloody chasm" by inviting them to a portion of the fatted calf. We intend of course to carve, and anticipate quite an accession to our ranks from this source, as quite a number here expressed themselves desirous of counseling with us for the welfare and prosperity of our new common country. We think the effect will be good, for it will show that we who fought for our country are as ready to forgive as they are to be forgiven.

Our convention, assembled for the purpose of sending delegates to Pittsburg, was large and enthusiastic, being the largest gathering of soldiers ever held here. We send fourteen delegates, all of them representative men. We shall instruct them to urge upon the Pittsburg Convention the propriety of holding Grant ratification meetings throughout the country upon some one day to be selected by the Convention. We think the effect would be grand, and will guarantee that the demonstration under our auspices will be the largest ever held on this coast.

I had the honor of being a delegate to the National Convention from this city, and it was my intention to have been present at the meeting of veterans called together at the Continental Hotel. As I was on this account unable to be present, Col. Coey's appointment was a good one. He is a gallant little fellow, and is well liked here. The Pacific coast will give her electoral votes to General Grant, California by 5,000 majority, Oregon 2,000, and Nevada 1,000 majority. These figures are reliable. Some of my Democratic friends admit them confidentially. We should be happy to hear from you, and to receive such information and advice as you may, from time to time, desire to give.

Respectfully yours,
CAPTAIN JAMES H. WITHINGTON,
Chairman Veterans' Executive Committee.

FROM REV. J. G. BUTLER, D. D.

WASHINGTON, D. C., September 22, 1872.

Col. L. E. DUDLEY, *Secretary, etc.*

Sir—In reply to yours, just handed me by my esteemed friend General James A. Ekin, U. S. A., so courteously communicating the request of the National Committee that I be present and act as chaplain of the National Mass Convention of Veterans, to be held at Pittsburg on the 17th inst., I regret that pending family bereavement necessarily detains me at home.

I appreciate the honor conferred by the committee, and, did the providence of God permit, I could not deny myself the privilege of meeting the veterans — representing the noble men who, under God, brought freedom and peace to the land—many of whom I have met in days darker and less hopeful than these. Our country is still safe in the keeping of the self-sacrificing men and women who saved it. Our honored chief has won no less the honor and confidence of the nation as our Executive than as the gallant and generous defender of our flag in the field. We who know him at home are pierced by the slanderous attacks upon his personal character. Modest, courteous, kind, patient amid abuse, going in and out among us as a man among men, regularly and devoutly hearing the Lord's Word on the Lord's Day, we honor and esteem him.

In the magnanimity of Christian patriotism, it is ours to heal and bind that which was rent by fraternal bondage and civil strife.

The varied nationalities and sectionalisms of this great people are yet to be welded by the educational and religious influences of our common Christianity. The school-book and the church for the common brotherhood, education for all, imbued with a gospel broad as the Word of God.

With an abiding faith in the triumph of truth, with an unfaltering confidence in the veteran survivors of many battles, and with an unswerving trust in the Lord Jehovah, our fathers' God, I pray that Heaven may guide your deliberations, and, in the future as in the past, give victory to the right.

Again thanking you for the kind invitation, and regretting my inability to be with you, I am, for God and our country.

Very truly yours,
J. GEO. BUTLER.

EXTRACTS FROM LETTERS RECEIVED.

The following are extracts from a few of the thousands of letters received in response to the call :—

Horatio Jenkins, late Colonel of the Fourth Massachusetts Cavalry, and Brevet Brigadier-General, writes :—

" As one of those who served under the banner of the Republic for three years in defense of the Union, I beg to assure you of my hearty approval of the call for a general convention of soldiers and sailors of the late war, to meet at Pittsburg, Penn., on the 17th of September next.

" I am sure the proposed convention will give such an expression of faith in the integrity of Gen.Grant, and in the principles of government it cost so many valuable lives to establish and to preserve during the late rebellion, as shall convince Liberal Republicans, Democrats, and Ku-Klux that the lies and slanders they have uttered against the President and his administration have only strengthened the enthusiasm of the veterans in support of the party that crushed the rebellion, and in support of the well-tried leader who has borne the standard of the Republican party ' full high advanced,' with no less courage, firmness, wisdom, and success in peace than in war."

Cornelius G. Attwood, of Boston, writes, under date of July 25th :—

" We organized yesterday, under the call of the Veterans' National Committee, for a convention at Pittsburg, Sept. 17th, with Gen. Horace Binney Sargeant in the chair. A committee of twelve prominent soldiers (with power to increase their number to 100) were elected to have entire charge of the ' On to Pittsburg' movement. The ball has been started, and will roll until we send off a very large delegation in September."

William Peterkin, late gunner United States Navy, writes :—

" Will you please place my name on your veteran list for Pittsburg. Let us again stand shoulder to shoulder, and victory will be ours in the future as in the past."

John H. Husted, late Company H, Ninety-fifth Regiment New York Volunteers, says :—

" As I am one of the many who responded to the call of duty in 1861, to defend our Republic and establish the principle that all should enjoy the inalienable right to life, liberty, and the pursuit of happiness, so I may be found now, with the same object in view, heartily responding to the call of your committee for a Veterans' Convention, to assemble in Pittsburg, Penn., on the 17th of September next."

John R. King writes from Baltimore as follows :—

" We had a large and enthusiastic meeting of soldiers and sailors on Tuesday night. Great interest was manifested, and the prospects are that a delegation numbering fully 250 men will go to Pittsburg. Some of our enthusiastic friends even estimate it at 400. I will send you a list of those who indorse the Pittsburg call next week; in the meantime send me some more blanks, so that I can send them through the State. We have another meeting next Tuesday evening, and propose keeping it up lively."

Gen. John T. Averill, the gallant cavalry commander, writes :—

" I have your favor of 16th inst., inviting me to be present at the Grand National Mass Convention of Veterans, to be held at Pittsburg, Penn., on the 17th of September next. In reply I have to say that I know of nothing now to preclude my attendance. I heartily rejoice to see the veteran element of our country aroused and zealous in the work. The blessed rights and privileges, procured at the cost of property and life, can only be maintained by keeping from power the hostile hands that opposed our efforts when the country was in peril."

Brevet Major-Gen. E. L. Molineaux, of New York, says :—

" I feel fully identified in any movement tending to the re-election of Gen. Grant, and shall heartily support in every way in my power the Republican nominations headed by Grant and Wilson."

F. C. Mann, formerly member of the Chicago Mercantile Battery, writes :—

" As one of the ' boys in blue' who participated in the war, and at the great demonstration in Pittsburg in 1866, I heartily give my support to the proposed reunion in September at that place. To my mind the people, and especially the veterans of the old army who carried the Stars and Stripes from Minnesota to Texas, should unite closer than ever to support our old and tried leader, U. S. Grant. *I cannot see that the old issues are dead.* I am not willing to have a change in affairs; therefore, gentlemen of the committee, I shall be pleased to meet you in September, and hope that we will triumphantly re-elect our old loved chieftain."

John S. Chandler, Company E, Seventy-fourth Illinois Regiment, writing from Shelbina, Mo., says:—

"I cannot see how any true soldier can desire to see the rebel Democracy restored to power, and this is exactly what the election of Greeley would accomplish; so you can put me down for one vote for Grant and the good old Republican party."

Col. Wm. Phelps, of Detroit, Mich., says:—

"We have the same foe before us that we had from 1861 to 1865, whipped—but unrepentant rebels and copperheads, to whom are united a few soreheads, all out of office, seeking it at all hazards and by all dishonorable means. Recent conversations and intercourse with late rebels from Mississippi, Louisiana, and other Southern States, who claim to accept the situation (only because they cannot help it), have led me to see the same spirit and desire they had in the rebellion, as I witnessed it, and who find a sympathy and fellow-feeling among the copperheads in our State, are the most abusive of our chief magistrate, and stoop to the most malignant slander. They were the most earnest in recommending Greeley's nomination and indorsing it. While the call of Johnson, Gordon, and other rebel generals, appear at the Baltimore Convention for the Confederates, North and South, to meet to consider the 'lost cause,' and how through Greeley they may regain it, the 'boys in blue,' in Michigan, will fall into line and stand by Grant as he stood by us and our country."

T. J. Downing. says:—

"I was a soldier of the late war; was at Antietam, a member of Company B, Sixtieth New York Regiment. For one I heartily approve of the call for a Veterans' Convention at Pittsburg, Sept. 17. St. Lawrence County furnished many soldiers, and, as they were for the Union then, so they are now."

Richard S. Tuthill, late Battery H, First Michigan Artillery, (Logan's old division), writes from Nashville, Tenn.:—

"There is no enthusiasm here among Democrats over the Tammany candidate, and all efforts to manufacture it have proved fruitless. For every weak-kneed Republican who votes for the Democrat—Greeley, Grant will gain ten votes in Tennessee from honest, sensible Democrats. I am satisfied that a thorough canvass will carry our State for Grant and Wilson.

Capt. W. M. Taylor, late Tenth United States Cavalry writes from Ottawa, Ill.:—

"As long as I see so many one-armed and one-legged men about me, as long as so many orphan children go about the streets, as long as so many widows mourn the loss of their husbands, *I don't propose to believe the issues of ten years ago are dead.* Neither do I propose to go for Horace Greeley, the man who is willing to forget every good he has done, and nullify his past record for the nomination of a mongrel Democratic 'loose' Republican sorehead Convention. Book me for Pittsburg, Sept. 17th, 1872."

A private letter from a distinguished ex-soldier from Fredericktown, Mo., says:—

"I hope to be able to meet those of our comrades who will be present at our National Convention at Pittsburg. on the 17th of September next, and I shall endeavor to secure the attendance of a large delegation from this State."

Capt. Clifford Coddington, Fifty-first New York Volunteers, who was severely wounded at the battle of Antietam, writes from Kingston:—

"It will afford me great pleasure to attend and to do anything in my power to advance the success of the proposed reunion. I believe with Horace Greeley, before he became a convert to Tammany, that 'Gen. Grant will be far better qualified for the presidential chair in 1872 than he was in 1868.'"

Gen. John L. Beveridge says:—

"I have received the kind invitation extended by the committee, through you, to be present and address the Convention of Soldiers and Sailors to be held at Pittsburg, Penna., on the 17th of September next, and thankfully accept the same."

Capt. Richard Carter, of Dodgeville, Wis., says:—

"I know of no soldier who has professed Republican principles who falters now."

A joint letter from Major Basbyschell, of the Forty-eighth Pennsylvania Volunteers, Wm. M. Runkle, of the Third Pennsylvania Artillery, and Charles Barlow, of the One Hundred and Twenty-first Pennsylvania Volunteers, says:—

"Heartily approving your call, dated the 5th inst., for a meeting of all soldiers and sailors who approve the nomination of Grant and Wilson, we respectfully ask that our names be enrolled as in every way indorsing the sentiments set forth in your call, pledging whatever influence we may possess in furthering the great cause of Republicanism pure and undefiled."

Col. James Luke and Major James B. Homer write:—

"We strongly favor the movement calling for a meeting of soldiers and sailors to indorse the renomination of Gen. U. S. Grant."

J. H. Stevenson, late private One Hundredth Pennsylvania Volunteers, says:—

"Under Republican rule during the past decade, our country has prospered beyond precedent, and if we have performed some of our duties slowly, it must be remembered we had to fight every inch of the way; our progress was at every step opposed by the bold, defiant and powerful organization known as the Democratic party; and although they have 'caved in' on almost all the points of difference, yet they have not 'come in.'"

THE DANGER OF A DEMOCRATIC VICTORY.

NEW HAVEN, CONN., July 6, 1872.

L. E. DUDLEY, Secretary Veterans' National Committee:

Dear Sir—The address of your committee meets my conviction of the duties the extraordinary crisis of the country devolves on the loyal men, who stood by the old flag and put down the rebellion.

The spectacle of a "new departure" that has taken such shape as to harmonize the Copperhead Democracy of the North and the rebel Democracy of the South with the so-called Liberal Republicans, headed by Mr. Greeley, is really cause of alarm. Should this departure succeed in the purpose of its leaders and break up the Republican party, it is not any unlike that our children would be testing on our old camp-grounds fighting again gigantic organized rebellion.

I am therefore the more earnest in my desire to see a full and fair expression of the sentiments of the veterans towards the present Chief Magistrate, and I think that their sentiments will have powerful influence with the honest millions of loyal people who have not yet forgotten their gratitude to that army and its illustrious chief who saved the Federal Union.

In my judgment, the re-election of President Grant at this crisis is quite as important to the country as his promotion to the supreme command of the army was in the darkest days of the rebellion. He conquered the rebellion then, he will preserve the costly results of its sacrifices now, if re-elected.

I am, sir, very respectfully,

B. S. ROBERTS,
Brevet Brigadier-General United States Army.

GREELEY ON EVERY SIDE OF EVERY QUESTION.

DETROIT, MICH., July 9, 1872.

My Dear General—Noticing in the press dispatches the call for a meeting of soldiers and sailors to endorse the action of the Philadelphia Convention, to be held at Pittsburg on the 17th of September, I take occasion to say that this movement has my most earnest sympathy.

The coming campaign will be one of great importance; as much so, perhaps, as any that has occurred since the foundation of the Government. The results of our four years of terrible war are at stake, and they can only be secured by the election of our old chief U. S. Grant. In my opinion, he has shown himself as great in managing civil affairs as in leading armies. Our country was never more prosperous and happy than under his administration. Our public obligations have been met ever before they were due. All our great financial interests feel that sense of security and permanence which they could not feel under a government presided over by that poor old vacillating demagogue, who has been on every side of every public question for the last thirty years.—Horace Greeley.

I shall endeavor to be in Pittsburg at the meeting, and shall be pleased to renew the associations so dear to me formed during nearly four years of active service in the late war. Wishing the movement the most complete success, I remain.   Yours very truly,

A. M. EDWARDS.
Late Colonel Twenty-fourth Michigan Infantry.

Gen. A. E. BURNSIDE. Fifth Avenue Hotel. New York.

Gen. JULIUS WHITE. of Chicago. says:—

"Please enroll my name as one of those who favor such an assemblage; and, if it be not out of place, let me now express the hope that the men who defended the country in its time of peril, will not deem our abandonment of the party, for whose principles they fought, a safe thing to do at present, if ever."

NOT READY FOR A REBEL COPARTNERSHIP.

WM. A. SCHMIDT, late Colonel of the Twenty-seventh Illinois Volunteers, and Brevet Brigadier-General. says:—

"I hereby inform you of my hearty indorsement and approval of the call for a Convention of Soldiers and Sailors on the 17th of September next, at Pittsburg, to ratify the nomination of our glorious leader, U. S. Grant, and his associate on the ticket, Henry Wilson. In the same month (September) six years ago, a similar convention met in the same place to condemn the attempted rule and prevent the transfer of the control of government from the hands of the grand Republican party to those of the Rebel Democracy. I had the honor and pleasure to be present at that Convention, as a delegate from the great State of Illinois. A similar attempt, in my opinion, is being made at this time, to place the country in the hands of those who would, if they could, have destroyed it. For one, I am not ready to sell out to rebels, or to even form a copartnership with Democrats; therefore, I propose to adhere to the principles for which I fought, and stand by the men with whom and under whom I stood in the fore-front of battle. Circumstances permitting. I shall be in Pittsburg."

STEALING UNION UNIFORMS.

E. P. HILL, late private First Marine Heavy Artillery. says:—

"I hope there will be a large attendance at Pittsburg, and shall be there if possible. This Greeley movement is simply the old rebel trick of stealing our uniforms."

WM. M. PERKINS says:—

"I hereby tender you the heart and hand of a 'high corporal,' desiring most earnestly to add my feeble effort for the furtherance of the glorious object in view, viz. the extirpation of the least and last remains of the rebellion from our midst, whether it comes from the Southern fire-eater or the Northern renegade. I believe that such results can only be achieved by the continuance in power of the present efficient administration, and I am one of many who hold the opinion that chaos and civil turmoil would follow the election of such a vacillating office-seeker as Horace Greeley to the head of this nation."

A VOICE FROM ANDERSONVILLE.

A. T. Decker, late Corporal Company L, Seventh New York Heavy Artillery, says:—

"In the campaign of 1864 I was taken prisoner at Cold Harbor, and was in Andersonville ten months. I weighed just ninety-six pounds when I came out of that fearful place, and I now feel no inclination to join hands with Horace Greeley and the rebels and copperheads who advocate his election. Let us re-elect Gen. Grant, and give Horace an opportunity to tell us more of 'what he knows' about farming, so that we may cultivate our 160 acres intelligently."

Joseph L. D. Riker, late private Company C, Fourteenth New York Volunteers, says:—

"I approve most heartily this call, and I thank you and those associated with you for your zeal in so good a cause. God bless our President."

Capt. John McGeehan says:—

"The men who both by land and sea followed the lead of such captains as Grant, Sherman, Sheridan, Farragut, Porter, Dupont, and others, who so nobly did their duty in their proper spheres, will not fail to do their whole duty by the country in its present crisis."

THE UNHOLY ALLIANCE.

E. L. Campbell, late Colonel Fourth New Jersey Volunteers, and Brevet Brigadier-General, says :—

"I have taken no active part in politics for six years past ; but the recent unholy alliance of our natural enemy with those who should be ashamed of the association makes me feel much like rendering such service as I may be able to do toward combating and defeating it. Please enroll me for Pittsburg."

Wm. Hemstreet, formerly Captain Eighteenth Missouri Volunteers, and Brevet Lieutenant-Colonel, says :—

"I have never held any civil office nor asked for any, and I am just as enthusiastically in favor of Gen. Grant's re-election as I was for his first election. I think for myself, as one of the people, and from the time I first met Grant on the mud-flats at Cairo, in 1861, until now, I have only unqualified admiration of him as a product of Americanism. I intend to fight his defamers, as I have from the first his enemies in front of him."

L. M. Tuxal, late private One Hundred and First Pennsylvania Volunteers, says :—

"I beg to state that, having been a soldier in the late war for four years, I most heartily approve of the movement and indorse the object thereof to the fullest extent."

Thomas Brown, late private Company D, Eighty-eighth New York Volunteers, says :—

"Please ' count me in ' in any undertaking your committee may think proper to commence in order to support Gen. Grant and his administration.'

A REBEL FLANK MOVEMENT.

Enos G. Burr, late private Eighteenth New Jersey Volunteers, says :—

"The nomination of Mr. Greeley by a few so-called ' Liberal Republicans' working for and in the interest of the Democratic party in its new departure, will avail nothing if we and our leaders are watchful and active; and if he is elected by men who have hated and cursed him for years, but who have now overcome and bound him upon the funeral-pile of political death, we to a certain degree will be responsible for the results. But it seems to me that the loyal men of the country cannot allow so great a change to come to pass. We must remember that it is our old enemy trying to flank us—Jeff. Davis and all united with him – to destroy our republic.

" Can any of our comrades so easily forget their brothers moldering under Southern soil from starvation, caused by unprincipled foes, and can they forget their own hardships in the work of overcoming that foe ?"

J. E. Morrison, late private Forty-sixth Ohio Volunteers, says :—

" I believe every soldier and sailor in Northwest Ohio will heartily indorse this cure. To my knowledge, there is not one Republican in this county supporting Greeley. The Democrats are sore at the proposed sale to be made at Baltimore on the 9th inst. With Greeley nominated, the Democratic party will be divided, and Grant, with every sail filled by a favoring breeze, will sail over the course triumphantly, and come to an anchorage in the White House again in November."

Private C. W. Hazzard says :—

"By all means let us have a bumper at Pittsburg ! Our experience of a former convention at the same place will warrant the going ahead with this. The Pittsburg boys will come right up with the work of getting ready and being ready, I am sure."

Jas. E. Montgomery, late Major and Assistant Adjutant-General United States Volunteers, says :—

" I hope to be able to be present at the meeting of soldiers and sailors to be held at Pittsburg on the next anniversary of the battle of Antietam, and shall do all in my power to induce others to unite in the movement."

STANDING BY THE OLD COMMANDER.

Private William McCarrick says :—

" I heartily approve the object of the call issued by your committee to the veterans of the late war, and I assure you it gives me the greatest pleasure to urge on all, and especially my former comrades, the necessity of standing by their old commander in this trying hour, instead of yielding the country to the hands of still unrepentant rebels."

Robert M. Davies, late Captain Sixty-second New York Volunteers, says:—

"As one of the veterans who served under Gen. Grant during the war, allow me to express my approval of the objects of the proposed Soldiers' and Sailors' Convention. I am as well satisfied with Gen. Grant's management of civil affairs as I am sure I was myself and all loyal men were, with the brave and gallant manner in which he gave the country peace. I, for one, shall stand under his banner and gladly hail him as my next President."

H. S. Hendee, late Surgeon One Hundred and Fifty-third New York Volunteers, says:—

"In common with those who served their country against treason and rebellion, I rejoice with my whole heart at the call for the Veterans' Convention at Pittsburg, Sept. 17th. It will have the presence of many, and the sympathy of all loyal men in the nation. The soldiers and sailors have no sympathy or respect for the vacillating advocate of Spiritualism, Fourierism, Brown-Breadism, Jeff. Davisism, Tammany-Hallism, and, finally, Whisky-Democracyism and his own isms besides; but they have confidence, sympathy, respect, and love for those 'who never faltered in our country's greatest danger,' and will heartily support the hero of a hundred battles and the honored and favorite son of the Republic, Gen. U. S. Grant."

Private C. W. Kilborn says:—

"Such an expression in favor of Grant and Wilson as will be given by the proposed convention must have its weight with the people, who still regard the wishes of those who for their sake and that of Republican principles placed themselves between them and all harm. The country trusted the army and navy then, and was saved. Has its faith and confidence in them ceased now? It cannot be."

Col. Gus. G. Frick, One Hundred and Twenty-ninth Pennsylvania Volunteers, answers:—

"Yes; let us have a general movement of the boys in the direction of Pittsburg. We hear in the distance the same old yell so many of us heard during 'the time that tried men's souls' on the other side of the Potomac and the Ohio, and it behooves us again to unfurl our flags, burnish up our arms, and prepare to meet the old, but disguised enemy. Let us throw out our skirmishers at Pittsburg, guard well against a 'pressure' from the rear, and then put the lines in motion, and keep moving until he is completely and finally vanquished. This is the feeling that pervades the ranks of the men in this direction who wore the blue, and who are now putting on their badges and mustering for the fight. An easy victory awaits us under our gallant leader, Gen. Grant, over the men who confronted us in the South, and those who fought for their country and flag north of the Susquehanna and Delaware, 500 miles away from danger."

W. W. Brown, late private First Pennsylvania Rifles, says:—

"The boys in blue never came together in any other than a good cause. They never have had, and I doubt if they ever will have, a relish for Tammany or Tammany candidates. They have a vivid recollection of 1863, when the army had to be divided in the most perilous hour of the Republic, in order to put down treason in New York. It is no satisfaction to know that Mr. Greeley has been faithful among the faithless; the question is, how does he stand now? That he leans upon 'Boss' Tweed for support is as plain as that he relies upon Trumbull. That Jeff. Davis is his supporter none can deny; and that they should go into the same political grave is quite appropriate; and that the soldiers should assist at the funeral is according to the eternal fitness of things."

Col. David Bronson, of Missouri, says:—

"I attended in 1866 a similar gathering as a delegate from Missouri, and propose to be present this year."

John Beverly, late Lieutenant-Colonel Thirty-fourth New York Volunteers, sends word:—

"I cannot see how any old veteran can adopt the rebel battle-cry of 'Anything to beat Grant.' This cry did not save the rebels, and it cannot save Greeley. I know of no old veteran that will vote for Greeley in this vicinity.".

Capt. W. D. Phillips says:—

"I heartily approve of the objects of the call for a great national meeting of soldiers and sailors who served the Union in her hours of trial."

Lieut. J. M. John, of Mount Carmel, Penna., says:—

"Our county, 'Northumberland,' will gladly respond, and send her delegates to confirm the majority that will be cast for our great leader in November."

Private Clifton W. Wiles, Tenth New York Cavalry, replies:—

"I cannot persuade myself that the men that promoted secession by their acts and words should yet be permitted to take control of a government which they endeavored to destroy and failed. The next election must be to them what Vicksburg and Gettysburg were to the Confederacy."

Sergt. F. J. Edwards, of Dowagiac, Mich., says:—

"Our picket-line in this community is still unbroken. We will march on the works of that man Greeley and send our votes with doubled interest to uphold the man who has done so well for our nation. *We love him and we will support him.*"

Major Henry O'Connor, late Attorney-General of Iowa, writes:—

"The call made by the committee for a convention of soldiers and sailors, to be held at Pittsburg on the 17th September next, meets with the warmest response from every soldier whom I have heard speak on the subject, and all desire to be there. I believe that at least 100,000 men from the old army and navy will be at Pittsburg on that day, all animated by a common purpose to manifest their love for the old flag, and to do honor to the man under whose lead that flag never was lowered. Gen. Grant's character needs no defense, either as soldier or civilian, general or magistrate; but, in the personal and coarse abuse which has been recently heaped upon him by rebels, copperheads, and soreheads, every soldier feels that he is himself insulted, and that, too, *because he was a soldier.*"

D. Anderson, late Colonel Nineteenth Michigan, says:—

"I know that the great mass of the soldiers and sailors that saved our country are sound to-day, and cannot be humbugged by any cry of corruption or reform coming from men so lately the open enemies of our country—or their friends. We want no such experiment. We *know* that under the present administration our country is safe, and we mean to keep it so."

Philadelphia, Penna., July 15, 1872.

L. E. DUDLEY, *Secretary Veterans' National Committee :*

Dear Sir—Noticing the call of your committee for a mass convention of the veteran soldiers and sailors of the late war, to meet in Pittsburg, on the 17th of September, I desire most heartily to indorse the same and express my sympathy with its objects, and I trust that the assembly call will bring together a body of veterans equal in numbers and enthusiasm with that which met in the same place and for a similar purpose in 1866.

With respect, very truly yours,

JAS. STEWART, Jr.,

Late Colonel Ninth New Jersey Volunteers, and Brevet Brigadier-General Commanding First Brigade, Second Division, Eighteenth Army Corps.

Col. A. P. Ketcham says:—

"You may put me down as one of those who approve the objects of your call *most emphatically.*"

John H. McMurdy, of Georgetown, Col., says:—

"As one of the soldiers from the Territory of Colorado, my name may be used to call the National Soldiers' and Sailors' Convention, and I am much mistaken if from every hamlet in the land there does not come the same spontaneous response."

PENNSYLVANIA SOLDIERS UNANIMOUS FOR GRANT.

W. C. Gray, of Chester, Penna., says:—

"We, the soldiers of Delaware County, Penn., are for U. S. Grant unanimously, without regard to former party prejudices, and in November will give the Grant electoral ticket the largest majority ever given for any ticket in this Republican stronghold."

William A. Short, late private Company E, Seventieth New York Volunteers, was secretary of the committee which organized the Convention of Soldiers and Sailors at Pittsburg, in 1866, and was removed from his place in the Treasury Department by Andrew Johnson for his labors at that time. The following extract from his letter shows that he still keeps up with the front line :—

"I send herewith a list of names of veterans who indorse the call for a soldiers' and sailors' convention, to be held in Pittsburg, Sept. 17, 1872, most of whom express their intention of attending the same. Our "boys in blue" in this section have not forgotten Greeley's "on to Richmond" one day, and "peace at any price" the next; nor his gratitude, afterward manifested by his uncalled-for opposition to the bill for equalizing the bounties, and his mean and bitter attacks upon those of the rank and file of the army who drafted the bill and advocated its passage as a matter of simple justice to the early volunteers. The Democratic party, both during and since the war, has been the implacable enemy of the Union soldier and sailor, and to support Horace Greeley now, the representative of that party, would be a stultification of every principle for which we contended in the field."

GRANT'S "SMOKING AND SUMMERING" IN VIRGINIA IN '64 AND '65.

Robert W. C. Mitchell, private Eighteenth New York Cavalry, says:—

" Having taken a hand in the war for the Union, I can hardly see how I cannot heartily approve of the objects of the call of the committee of which you are chairman. I trust the boys will awake to the fact that the enemy is up again, disguised, and now joined by cowardly deserters. Among the names attached to the call I noticed the names of men that I, with others, have followed in the fight against a brave Southern rank and file, and I am sure we cannot but join in the thrashing about to be given the valiant (?) home guards of '61 and '65—those who with Horace Greeley cried "on to Richmond," four hundred miles away, and fought and won the great battles of the war—on paper—while Grant was smoking and summering it down in Virginia, around such watering-places as Petersburg. Sound the reveille! Let's hammer hell out of them this time.

Brevet Major H. A. Norton, of Chicago, says:—

"The address of the Veterans' National Committee of July 5 meets with my hearty approval, and I firmly believe that great good will result from the meeting proposed. If possible, I shall be present Sept. 17th, and I believe that the old rank and file will still present an unbroken front to the enemy."

A. T. Johnson, of Kewanee, Ill., writes:—

" There are soldiers and sailors, and good Republican citizen voters enough, and a large majority over, to re-elect Gen. Grant, and we are going to do it this fall."

Private T. Jones, late Company F, Twelfth Pennsylvania, writes:—

" Agreeably to the invitation extended through the papers to the soldiers and sailors who favor the re-election of Gen. Grant as our next President, to meet in general convention at Pittsburg, Sept. 17th, I hereby notify your committee that I will be at the place appointed, if alive." The above was indorsed as follows : " We also heartily approve of this call, and signify our intention of being present at the Convention."

HENRY ABBOTT,
H. D. BUNSING,
SAM'L SEBLERY,
PETER TIPPENS.

FROM GENERAL W. W. BELKNAP, SECRETARY OF WAR.

WAR DEPARTMENT, WASHINGTON CITY, September 10, 1872.

*Dear Sir—*I have delayed answering your letter of invitation to the Grand National Convention of Soldiers and Sailors at Pittsburg, in the hope that I might be able to give you the assurance that I would be present ; and it is with much regret that I find myself compelled, by the pressure of official duties here, to decline the invitation.

But, though not permitted to be present with you, I cannot forego the opportunity of expressing to you my gratification at the spirit which has prompted the call for this Convention. At a time when party strife has made our opponents forget the eminent services during the war of the man who so often led us to victory, it is most fitting that his old comrades in arms, associates on many fields, should meet together in enthusiastic gatherings, to remind the republic that his achievements are not forgotten by those who, under his leadership, saved it from destruction.

It is not for me to recount his services. They are recorded in our hearts and in the history of our country. Those who know him have no fear that the Government will not be well conducted, if placed in his hands for another term. His administration of it for the past four years has been marked by a steady decrease of the public debt, by increased confidence in public credit, and by just and upright execution of the laws. A wise and steady policy in the same direction is the assurance to be derived from the experience of the past.

With a cordial greeting to all, and with my best wishes for a most pleasant meeting,

I am, very truly yours,
WM. W. BELKNAP.

L. E. DUDLEY, Esq., Secretary, etc., New York.

FROM GENERAL H. H. WELLS, EX-GOVERNOR OF VIRGINIA.

RICHMOND, VA., September 4, 1872.

Col. L. E. DUDLEY, *Secretary, etc.*:

Sir—Your letter, asking me to be present and address the Mass Convention of Soldiers and Sailors at Pittsburg on the 17th of this month, is at hand. While compelled by duties here to decline your invitation, I cannot willingly forego the opportunity of expressing my earnest approval and cordial sympathy with the great enterprise in which our comrades are engaged.

On the day that General Grant joined the army of the Potomac, to assume for the first time the command of it, I went with him to General Meade's headquarters. On the way between Manassas Junction and Brandy Station, the General said: "What do you think would be the consequence of electing as President, at this time, General McClellan, or any other Democrat?" I answered, "That it would, in my judgment, inevitably result in the early recognition of the independence of the Confederate States." His reply was: "*It could not be otherwise. This war must be successfully closed up, and the Republican party alone can be trusted with the responsibility of settling its issues.*"

What our great captain said then is true now. And I believe that General Grant's re-election is as vital to the great interests of the country as was the re-election in 1864 of our martyred leader, hero, and patriot—Abraham Lincoln.

Glorious to our armies, and honorable to the foes that opposed us, as was the surrender at Appomattox, neither General Grant's work, nor that of the Union soldiers, was there ended. It remained for him to protect the brave men who had already surrendered, and to secure for them the peaceful enjoyment of the just and magnanimous terms he had promised; but it remained as well for him and us to secure for the common benefit of the whole country—the South as well as the North—the precious fruits of the great battle that was won.

Good government is not yet fully established. The supremacy of the law is not everywhere maintained, nor do all the citizens possess the same full, bounteous measure of rights and privileges; the same just equality, nor the same ample protection and security for the safety of their persons, the enjoyment of their estates, or the free expression of their opinions; and, until this has been accomplished, our work will not be done.

The men who sought to defeat Abraham Lincoln and the Union army in 1864, seek to defeat General Grant and the Republican party in 1872. The weapons are not the same, but the consequences involved in a defeat now are quite as disastrous as then; and, in my judgment, a surrender to Mr. Greeley would be more dishonorable than a defeat by General Lee.

The Union men of the South appreciate the fact that the campaign of 1872 means for them a fierce and unremitting battle for existence against a foe that is unscrupulous, remorseless, and brutal.

We know that the party represented by Mr. Greeley treats all men in the South, not acting and voting with it, as enemies who are entitled to none of the rights secured by the rules of civilized warfare, but to be mercilessly persecuted, and cruelly punished for what is no crime under the constitution of God or civil society. It denounces all Republicans as either "niggers," "carpet-baggers," or "scalawags," and every one of each class as an outlaw and a scoundrel, to be hunted down by paid spies, tried on the testimony of suborned witnesses, and condemned by packed juries and partisan judges.

It regards the negro as not fit for the rights, nor entitled to the privileges of citizenship, and, therefore, to be speedily remitted to a worse condition of ignorance and degradation than that in which he has heretofore been kept, which can best be done by abolishing constitutional provisions adopted for his protection, closing the public schools, excluding him from the jury-box, even when his own race is on trial, and by the general re-establishment and frequent use of the whipping-post.

It regards every native of the State, no matter what his lineage, virtue, patriotism, standing, or character, if he is a Republican, as a proper subject to be assailed, abused, and defamed, threatened, intimidated, and persecuted; banished from society, cut off from his former friends, and degraded in the public estimation to the last degree of human endurance.

The same infamous party creed is not less cruel nor remorseless towards the citizen who comes here from another State. If an active Republican, no matter how long he has been here, how extensive his possessions, how unblemished his character, how useful his enterprises, or how permanent his attachment to the State, he is to be excluded from society, denied the courtesies of civilized life, treated as an intruder, derided as an enemy, harassed with vexations, prosecutions, and accused of crimes of which he is not guilty, until he either changes his politics, leaves the State, or his ostracism, persecution, and oppression are ended in a prison, or possibly in a dungeon, with a halter at the end of it.

Governed by such a creed, and ruthlessly executing so barbarous a policy, there is no necessity of Ku-Klux, or any other secret association of cut-throats or midnight assassins; the cost of their paint, disguises, and dark lanterns, is an unnecessary expense and a useless waste of money.

There are in the South a multitude of men and women born here, too just, too patriotic and humane to believe in, defend, or justify the monstrous creed to which I have referred; but, with Horace Greeley as a leader of his present following, and a successful presidential candidate, such good men and women become utterly powerless to stay the tide of disaster, oppression, suffering, and sorrow, which even now threatens us.

I had occasion to express these same sentiments about a year since, nor has the year passed in any degree abated the confidence then entertained in the truth of the statements made, nor weakened the apprehensions then felt of the great and impending danger that now threatens the South.

The Republican party and General Grant, and not Mr. Greeley, are the authors of every measure of justice and wise liberality which has been extended to the South since the close of the war; amnesty, peace, and fraternity is their pledged policy for the future; and not until the great principles of justice and equality are put into active operation, will the mission of the Republican party, or the duty of the Union soldier be ended; the defeat of General Grant now would re-open all the healed wounds and inaugurate an administration disastrous to the whole country—unfortunate for the North, and cruel to the South. The soldiers who have lain down their muskets and sabres, must now take up their ballots and vote as they fought, until all men are indeed equal, and so secure in their equalities, that they can express their opinions and vote for the candidates of their choice in the South as freely and with as little fear of ostracism, threats, or intimidations, as they can in the North to-day.

I hope and believe that the Convention will be a great success, that General Grant will be re-elected, and by the largest majority ever given to a presidential candidate, and that, by a wise, firm, and patriotic administration of public affairs, the whole country will indeed be blessed; and that while the North rejoices in rights secured, the South will hail General Grant as the great pacificator, the chieftain, and leader, who won his best triumphs by a great victory over their worst prejudices.

I remain, my dear sir, very sincerely yours,

H. H. WELLS.

RECEPTION OF THE VETERANS AT PITTSBURG, PA.

Never before, in the history of this country, have such unusual and magnificent preparations been made for the reception and entertainment of any assemblage, as was made upon this occasion by the people of Pittsburg. Nearly every house in that city was decorated with flags, banners, and mottoes. At the crossings of all the principal streets, triumphal arches, covered with evergreens and flowers, were erected. At nearly every private house in the entire city the doors were thrown open to receive the many thousand guests who were unable to be entertained at the hotels. At the City Hall tables were spread, bounteously loaded with tempting viands, and in one day the noble-hearted women of Pittsburg fed at those tables over fourteen thousand soldiers.

During the entire session of the Convention every prominent street in the city was so entirely filled with people as to be almost impassable. They came in a manner that would have delighted the great heart of the Martyr-President. They came as the heroic sons of the nation did, when he called for them to come with their lives in their hands to save its integrity and insure its perpetuity. They came from the humble cottages among the valleys of the Monongahela and Allegheny; from the workshops, the foundries, and the mines. They came "as the winds come when navies are stranded," in the grandeur and glory of their might.

On Tuesday evening speeches were delivered to immense audiences by men of national reputation, at more than twenty different places in the cities of Pittsburg and Allegheny. The enthusiasm was unbounded; cheers, songs, and instrumental music filled the air during the entire night, and it seemed as if all had abandoned any thoughts of sleep, and had given themselves up to the full enjoyment of the occasion. On Wednesday morning the grand daylight procession was formed; this was composed almost entirely of the Republicans of Pittsburg and Western Pennsylvania, intended for the purpose of welcoming the veterans of the nation to their locality; words fail to convey any adequate idea of the magnificence of this display. The procession was exactly two hours and a half in passing a given point, and it was estimated that more than ten thousand men were in the line. Persons who had the opportunity to observe this grand display, expressed the opinion that it was the finest demonstration of the kind ever seen in the country. They saw only immense wagons bearing emblems, the municipal and rural industries of Allegheny, some fantastic bodies of men, mounted delegations, and an infinite variety of people intending to participate, first moving in confusion through the streets, and a little while later evolving out of this chaos, like a huge anaconda of infinite proportions unrolling itself, as a great long column of people in vehicles of every kind, embowered in evergreens, covered with flags, amidst the most grotesque, suggestive, and indescribable associations—the whole pageant passing, in well-ordered but vivacious procession, through the principal streets of both cities.

The procession marched over the prescribed route, amid the plaudits of one hundred thousand spectators, to Friendship Grove, a magnificent cluster of forest trees on the outskirts of the city, where it disbanded for the purpose of listening to speeches from Gens. B. F. Butler, E. F. Noyes, and many others.

The torchlight procession of Wednesday evening was the most brilliant ever witnessed in that city. The line was more than ten miles long, and was over three hours in passing a given point. An eye-witness has described it as follows; but, to be appreciated, it should have been seen:—

"Rome was an ocean of flame"—and so was Pittsburg last evening. The appearance of the city during the early hours, before the illumination began, was most inspiriting. Every street was jammed with people, all wending their way as rapidly as possible to the centre of attraction—Fifth avenue. Almost every building was adorned with flags, mottoes, and transparencies, and nearly all prepared for the illumination at a later hour. But the climax was reached about seven o'clock. At that hour, Fifth avenue, which had been reposing in the glare of a dozen or two of street-lamps, seemed as though Plantamour's comet had suddenly swept over it, leaving its lustre behind; thousands of flame-jets, of all colors, suddenly flashed upon the scene, revealing the thoroughfare in all its wondrous beauty, and evoking long-continued plaudits from the one hundred thousand people who were thronging it. A few minutes past seven the Ninth Ward and Elizabethborough clubs—*avant-couriers* of the grand army of torch-bearers—essayed the passage of the avenue, as if to test the practicability of forcing a passage through the dense masses of people. As they moved slowly along, holding aloft their blazing torches, they were greeted with tumultuous cheering, while red, white, and blue flames, rockets, Roman candles, etc., cast a weird-like effulgence over the avenue and adjacent streets. At a later hour the grand procession began to move over the prescribed route, when the same scenes were repeated, only, if possible, they were intensified.

It was a grand success. There was no blundering, no confusion. Competent men had prepared the plan, and willing hands executed it. It was creditable to the city. The fame of the grand display will be heralded all over the nation, and people will learn that the heart of the "Iron City" beats responsive to every sentiment of hospitality, and that nowhere are the "soldiers and sailors held in higher esteem."

Of the untiring efforts and lavish expenditure of time and money by the citizens of Pittsburg to prepare a glorious welcome for their veteran visitors, too much cannot be said. Every soldier and sailor who was present has engraved upon his heart the kindest remembrance of the hospitality of the city whose walls and clouds are ever black, but the hearts of whose people are ever warm. If anything can repay a man for the pain of wounds and disease endured in the field, far away from the loved ones at home, it is such hearty welcomes as were accorded them by the noble, kind-hearted men and women of Allegheny County.

THE CONVENTION.

TUESDAY, SEPTEMBER 17, 1872.

THE CONVENTION CALLED TO ORDER.

After the singing of a "Song of Welcome" by the Welsh Glee Club of Pittsburg, and the "Star Spangled Banner" by a chorus composed of about one hundred singers from the Pittsburg choirs, under the leadership of Prof. W. J. Polk, Major Samuel Harper, of Pittsburg, at 11 o'clock, A. M., called the Convention to order, and said:—

REMARKS OF MR. HARPER.

COMRADES—I have the honor to introduce to you, for the purpose of extending to you the hospitality of Pittsburg, our fellow comrade, General J. B. Sweitzer.

ADDRESS OF WELCOME.

General Sweitzer said :—

COMRADES—In the name, and on behalf of the citizens of Pittsburg, and of the State of Pennsylvania, I bid you welcome among us.

I greet you as the representatives of those hosts of valiant patriots, who at the call of their country went forth to battle for her honor and her flag.

With the trials of war now over, and in the full enjoyment of the glorious results—a nation saved and reunited, with all its people free—it is pleasant to come together again—to keep up the memory of past events, to thank the Providence that has carried us, comparatively unharmed, through years of fiery trial, and to drop a tear over those whom the same Providence had appointed to die, in order that a great nation might live. What recollections throng upon us, as we look back to that day—but little more than eleven years since—when the blow struck at our country's flag by a traitor's hand thrilled like an earthquake shock through the length and breadth of our land, and the streets of our cities rocked under the tread of a million of men who were in arms to avenge it, when the strife was, not who should be excused, but only who should find a place in the ranks of its defenders.

Among the earlier of the more important engagements of the war was the battle of Antietam, on the anniversary of which we meet to-day. It occurred just ten years since, in the darkest hour of the Republic. The campaign of the Peninsula had terminated disastrously, and the Army of the Potomac had been withdrawn. The Army of Virginia, under Pope, had been checked and driven back across the Rappahannock, and to the very gates of Washington, and the 1st of September, 1862, saw both these armies shattered and disordered behind the fortifications of the Capital. Such was the condition of the Union forces in the East when the invasion of Maryland was resolved upon, and commenced by Lee—and in the prosecution of this design the battles of South Mountain and Antietam were fought.

In them the old Army of the Potomac [applause] won some of its brightest laurels ; and in the latter, which was one of the greatest conflicts of the war, it gained its first victory in a general engagement over the adversary against which it had so long contended.

To refer to its incidents in detail—to describe the fierce struggles on the right, under Hooker [cheers], and Meade [cheers], and Mansfield, and Williams, and Sumner, and Franklin—the taking and retaking of the corn-field and the lands beyond, four times lost and won, the storming of the bridge on the left under Burnside [long-continued cheers]—carried at the point of the bayonet, in a charge led by that gallant Pennsylvanian, General John F. Hartranft [loud applause], then Colonel of the 51st Pennsylvania Volunteers, and the desperate conflict that ensued and continued until nightfall—would require more time than I am allowed on this occasion.

It can only be referred to, as a whole, as one of the most momentous battles of the war

—in the magnitude of the armies engaged, and in the valor displayed by both officers and men—attested as it is by the fearful loss of life and the casualties on either side. Near two hundred thousand men and five hundred pieces of artillery were engaged for fourteen hours —from the first dawn of the morning till darkness enveloped the earth and ended the carnage, and then more than twenty-five thousand of these brave men lay dead and wounded on that sanguinary field. The Army of the Potomac held the ground their valor had wrested from the enemy, and was thus far declared the victor.

And here ended the battle of Antietam. It was not renewed on the morning of the 18th. The troops of both armies spent the day in removing the wounded and burying their dead. The morning of the 19th was anxiously looked forward to as the time when the bloody strife would again begin ; but, alas ! the dawn of that morning revealed the fact that Lee, with his shattered legions, had recrossed the Potomac under cover of darkness, and was again on the soil of his native Virginia. Thus ingloriously terminated this bold and desperate attempt of the rebel chieftain to get to the rear of Washington, to sweep victoriously on to the Susquehanna, and then return and besiege Baltimore and the National Capital.

Its results had been disastrous to him in the extreme. His supplies were exhausted. His army was dispirited, shattered, and disorganized. His losses, since he entered Maryland, a fortnight before, were nearly thirty thousand men, and although his whole army was not captured, or ruined, as subsequent events have shown it might possibly have been, it is nevertheless certain that the failure of this campaign was the severest blow the rebel cause had yet received. A word as to the character of the contest in which you were all lately engaged.

The exciting cause had long existed. Its origin dated far back in the history of our country, even to its very beginning as a nation. In the constitution of the wisest and best government God ever gave to man, our fathers made but one mistake. They found an institution here at war with the great rights of humanity, and with the very first utterances of their own sublime and immortal declaration ; and they could see no alternative but to accept it under the conviction. no doubt, that under the will of Providence and the influence of free institutions it would die; at all events, as it has just now done. They did not, however, anticipate that it was to go out in a convulsion that would rend the nation and desolate so many happy homes by carrying its children to the sacrifice, and dye its fields with such rivers of fraternal blood. It was this tolerance of evil that proved our only source of strife. It was in the very nature of things impossible that the conflicting principles of human equality and property in man should flourish side by side. It could not be otherwise than that the idea of ownership in the thews and sinews of labor should have a tendency not only to degenerate labor itself, but to change the character of society, to engender pride, and arrogance, and aristocratic feeling, and distinction of caste, and to induce it to look down upon the hardy sons of toil—the dwellers in the Free States, as an inferior race, unfit either to govern States or to encounter them in the field.

It was no longer a question between the black man and the white, nor between those who thought there was an argument for the toleration of slavery and those who thought otherwise. It was a question whether the arrogant and supercilious white men of the South, who affected to despise the men of the free States, should be allowed to rend and destroy the Union—that last hope of freedom to man, which had been cemented by the blood of our fathers upon many a hard-fought field. It was a direct challenge to every lover of liberty among us, whatever might have been his politics, to vindicate the right of self-government by showing his ability to defend it with the sword, if necessary. It was a test-question. The world stood waiting on the issue. The friends of liberty everywhere trembled, and the advocates of arbitrary power exulted as the scales hung doubtful in the opening of the conflict. The freemen of the North could not decline to meet it, and they did meet it in such way as to settle that question to the confusion of the enemies of free government forever. The world has seen nothing like the answer which they made. It was a million of men in arms, and a million more if necessary. It was the last dollar and the last drop of blood, if the nation had wanted both for that tremendous conflict. The conflict is now over, and the root of bitterness, the germ of civil discord, is removed. We have weathered the only headland that could have threatened us with shipwreck. From the mighty struggle that strained our sinews to their utmost tension, we have come up with a new life, and a development of strength that has astonished the world and ourselves, and put us at the head of the great powers of Christendom, with a now cloudless sky above us, that foretells a career of greatness, not in arms only, but in the arts of industrial life also, far beyond anything the world has ever seen.

Was not all this worth the sacrifice ? Yes, even the sacrifice, great as it may have seemed. Of those who died, a nation saved will be the monument so long as time endures.

What hero of the past rests in a prouder mausoleum, or has done a work so great for humanity as this? The dead, in such a strife, are scarcely to be mourned—for theirs is a crown of imperishable life. If they are not here to-day, it is only because the glories of martyrdom were reserved for them, while we are left to share with others the fruits of their great struggle. Honor to their memories!

To you who survive, it would be presumptuous in me to undertake to rehearse the stories of your marches, your bivouacs, and your battles—of your toils, your sufferings, and your sacrifices, during the years you gave to the redemption of the nation. To do so would require a recital of the history of the war. Their stories are already written, and will be read by your children as a lesson and an example.

It only remains for me to express the wish that your visit may be pleasant and profitable; that your action while here may contribute, materially, to the maintenance of the principles and objects for which you fought, and to the vindication of the Great Captain who led you to victory, and who, at the head of the nation, has been as true, efficient, and successful, as he was at the head of its armies in the field. And, my comrades, may you long survive to enjoy the consciousness of duty well performed, and the peace you have so honorably earned.

During the applause which followed General Sweitzer's remarks, General John W. Geary, Governor of Pennsylvania, accompanied by General Ambrose E. Burnside, of Rhode Island, Chairman of the National Committee, appeared on the stage, and both were received by long-continued cheers, which were renewed again and again. When silence was secured, Governor Geary spoke as follows:—

SPEECH OF GOVERNOR GEARY.

Comrades, Ladies, and Gentlemen—Although it is not in the programme, still, my friends, our worthy President has called upon me this morning, and within a few moments, to extend to you a few further words of welcome than those contained in the address of General Sweitzer. I most cordially indorse all that was said in that excellent address, and I may say to you that I most gladly appear here this morning for the purpose of meeting, face to face, so many of the familiar faces that I have met in times of trial and great difficulty—in the throes of this nation. I am glad to meet you as a citizen; secondly, as a comrade; thirdly, as the Chief Magistrate of the great State of Pennsylvania. [Applause.] I come before you this morning in the name of the great commonwealth of Pennsylvania—the State in which the Declaration of Independence was first promulgated—where the bell first rang out "freedom to the inhabitants of the earth!" I come before you in the name of a State that has been a State of freedom and of men who were ever ready to bare their breasts for the protection of this glorious Union. I come before you in the name of the State that gave 366,000 soldiers for the preservation of the Union. [Applause.] I feel, indeed, when I hear those cheers, my friends, that I am in the presence of comrades that gave the good old-fashioned cheer, and not the wolfish howl of the rebel. [A voice—"No rebel yell here."] I am here for a purpose, and I don't intend to detain you but for a moment. I stand in the presence of soldiers from all parts of this Union, who have come here to-day in order to greet a great and illustrious chieftain. [Applause.] I feel that you have come here to-day to welcome another hero of the war, comrades—Major-General John F. Hartranft. [Applause.] My friends, I do not wish to detain you here long. I have a few more words to say. [Cries of "Go on, go on."] I thank Almighty God that he has preserved so many of us to meet again on the soil of this good old State, where we may renew the friendships that were formed on the march, in the bivouac, and on the field of battle. I come to extend to you, on behalf of the State I represent, a most sincere, cordial, and hearty welcome to the good old commonwealth of Pennsylvania. I assure a hearty welcome to each and every one of you. Welcome, soldiers and preservers of this Union to Pennsylvania soil! yea, a thrice hearty welcome to all of you. I commit you to the care of my fellow-citizens of Pittsburg. I feel that they will give you a hearty welcome, and cause it to be long remembered that the soldiers of the nation convened upon this day—the tenth anniversary of the battle of Antietam—that did so much for the preservation of the Union and the breaking down of the rebellion. [Applause.] I hope that your sojourn among us will be as pleasant and agreeable to you as it will be to us. I trust that our meeting will be one that shall be long remembered in the heart of every true and patriotic soldier in this Union.

I trust that everything will be done here that will advance the cause in our coming struggle, a cause in which our hearts are so deeply engaged. We feel that this is a conflict above all others, my friends, which should determine the great questions growing out of the war. The people of the South and the sympathizers with the rebellion during the war are getting up every year some new questions that are to be brought before us, to show that the questions of the war shall not be settled. We want to gather and march together in solid column, and produce such a result as will cause that question to be forever settled. In this glorious struggle we ever intend to meet them face to face. We will make it such a Waterloo, such a Gettysburg, that they—[A voice "Set Iowa down for 50,000 majority for Grant;" another voice—"Set Virginia down for 10,000 majority for Grant"]—will never do so again. New Hampshire has spoken, and we have heard from Connecticut; the Green Mountain boys have spoken, and they have told us in tones of thunder that they intend to preserve the fruits of victory. [A voice—"New York will put on a top-dressing of 20,000."] We have heard from Maine, and she has given such a majority as will make assurance doubly sure. A few weeks ago, when I was in New York, they told me New York was good for 80,000 for Greeley. Now they tell me the city cannot give him more than 10,000 or 15,000. [A voice—"The little Democratic State of New Jersey will roll up a majority of 10,000 for Grant."] And I begin to think, my friends, that the oldest encyclopedia of all the isms of the country may possibly receive the vote of Kentucky. [Great applause.] [A voice—"We spoke from North Carolina last month."] Gentlemen and comrades, I reiterate my welcome—a thrice hearty welcome. [A voice—"The possum policy will bury Gratz Brown, Frank Blair, and Carl Schurz forever beneath the snow-drifts."] I will add one word more to my Missouri friend's expression—*we will all go to the funeral.* [Laughter and applause.]

On the conclusion of Governor Geary's address, General Burnside appeared, and was greeted with rounds of applause, cheers being also given for "Little Rhody." Quiet having been restored, General Burnside introduced Rev. William Preston, of Pittsburg, who offered the following prayer:—

PRAYER.

O, Thou great Author of Creation! we rejoice to call Thee our Heavenly Father. Unto Thee shall all flesh come; and we rejoice, our Heavenly Father, at the privilege of drawing nigh to Thy throne of grace, in the name of our Divine Redeemer, with the assurance that if we come in his name, and acknowledge Thee in all our ways, Thou wilt direct our paths. We trust in Thy infinite mercy in Christ Jesus. We rejoice that Thou art the Lord our God, the God of our fathers, the God of our country, and the God of all flesh. We rejoice in Thy precious Word, and in the atoning sacrifice of Thy Son; that Thou hast so loved the world as to give Thine only-begotten Son, that whosoever believeth on him might not perish, but have everlasting life. We thank Thee for all Thy blessings, for all Thy mercies; for the prosperity and peace in all our borders, and for the friendly relations which prevail between our country and all foreign lands. We thank Thee for the abundant harvests of the season, and for the prosperous condition of the nation in all its commercial and financial interests. We thank Thee that Thou hast spared us from the pestilence which walketh in darkness, from the destruction which wasteth at noon-day. All these, Father of Mercies, are Thy good and perfect gifts; and we call upon our souls and all that is within us to praise and magnify Thy glorious name, praying that Thou wouldst give us that peace and blessing that Thou givest to all Thy servants. We beseech Thee give us hearts to appreciate Thy goodness and mercies, and help us to live no more unto ourselves and unto the world, but unto Him who died for us and rose again.

Now, our Heavenly Father, we pray that Thou wouldst hold in favor and bless Thy servant, the President of these United States, and all others in authority, and so replenish them with the grace of Thy holy Spirit, that they may always incline to Thy will and walk in Thy ways. Endue them with Thy holy Spirit, that Thy great name shall be glorified in all their ways. Bless, also, we beseech Thee, the soldiers and sailors of our own country, and the widows and orphans of those who have passed away, and are to be seen among us no more. May they never be forgotten in the prayers, sympathies, and kindness of the nation; and to all of us give Thy heavenly grace, that we may know and do all our duty to Thee, to our country, and to our fellow-men.

Bless us, especially, our God, in the forgiveness of all our sins, and with those spiritual blessings in Christ Jesus, which are the foretaste and pledge of our everlasting salvation. Bless this Convention now assembled here; guide them in all their deliberations. May wisdom from on high enlighten every mind, and the spirit of true holiness reign in every heart, that whatsoever is done may be begun, continued, and ended in Thee, so Thy great name may be glorified in all things, through Jesus Christ, our glorious Redeemer.

Our Father which art in heaven, hallowed be Thy name; Thy kingdom come; Thy will be done on earth as it is in heaven. Give us this day our daily bread, and forgive us our trespasses, as we forgive them that trespass against us. Lead us not into temptation, but deliver us from evil, for Thine is the kingdom, the power, and the glory, for ever. Amen.

Gen. Burnside then formally called the Convention to order, and spoke as follows:—

SPEECH OF GENERAL BURNSIDE.

COMRADES—While in attendance as a delegate to the National Republican Convention in Philadelphia, it was suggested to me that it would be proper for veterans of the late war to assemble in mass convention, to express their views upon the political questions which are now agitating the country. Knowing as I did that the soldiers and sailors of the Union army entered the service of their country from patriotic motives, and, when their work was completed, returned to their peaceful pursuits without discord or commotion, and became quiet, peaceful citizens, and that their opinions would be respected, I at once joined heartily in the movement.

A meeting of those who were attending the Philadelphia Convention, and who had been identified with the army and navy of the Union, was called, and a National Committee of Veterans was appointed for the purpose of arranging for this grand mass convention, and this day, as a memorable anniversary, was named as the day of meeting. I had the great honor of being named as the chairman of that committee; and I now appear before you, comrades, to complete the duties which devolved upon me, by calling your Convention to order and naming to you a temporary chairman.

It is quite unnecessary for me to say to you that, in making arrangements for this Convention, the main part of the work necessary to its success, and to your comfort and happiness, has been done by the local committees, and the loyal men and women of Pittsburg and vicinity. [Applause.] You can all bear testimony to the great service which has been performed by Col. L. E. Dudley, the Secretary of the National Committee.

Comrades, you have before you a great duty to perform, second only to that which devolved upon you when you left your homes to battle for the preservation and integrity of the nation. It is but a few short years since you returned to your peaceful pursuits, and you now find yourselves confronted by a formidable coalition, composed of bad and weak men, who were either in open hostility to the authority of the Government, or in active sympathy with the enemies of their country during the time of its greatest trouble. [Applause.]

This combination has been enhanced in numbers by the desertion of a few disappointed, discontended, and dilapidated men who acted with the Republican party during the war, and a large majority of whom have been heavy weights upon the Republican party ever since. [Laughter and applause.]

I had, during the war, a slight personal experience, which illustrates the course which these men pursued. All my comrades of Western Pennsylvania, Ohio, and Indiana will remember that I was compelled by a sense of duty to arrest Mr. Vallandigham [loud applause] for treasonable conduct during the war. You will also remember that I gave him fair warning by issuing General Order No. 38. In disregard of that order, he continued to counsel resistance to the authority of the Government, and was therefore arrested. Mr. Lincoln, in the kindness of his heart, urged me to release Mr. Vallandigham, and gave me the names of distinguished citizens who had told him that I had made a very serious mistake in making the arrest, and that Mr. Vallandigham would be considered as a martyr, and that the political enemies of the Administration in Ohio would at once make him their standard-bearer as a candidate for Governor, and elect him by an overwhelming majority. [Shouts of "Never!" "They did not do it," etc.] I represented to Mr. Lincoln that I was upon the ground and knew the situation better than those gentlemen, and that Mr. Vallandigham would not be released unless superior authority so ordered. [Applause.] Mr. Lincoln said to me that he would not interfere, but had simply given advice at the instance of prominent citizens. Among these was Mr. Trumbull, of Illinois. [Groans and hisses.] What was the result of this decision of Mr. Lincoln declining to interfere, as he was urged to do by Mr. Trumbull and others? Mr. Vallandigham was put forward as a candidate and was beaten by that gallant old war-horse, Gov. Brough, by over one hundred thousand majority. [Immense applause.] The action of the people of Ohio at that time demonstrated their loyalty to the Government, and I doubt not that their action in the present campaign will quite as strongly illustrate it. [Applause, and cries of "It will!"]

I will not detain you, comrades, by discussing the political questions of the day. You will have them fully discussed by other people who are skilled in public debate; besides, I am quite satisfied that you are all fully posted upon such topics. Men that have served in the field, and staked their lives upon an issue so important to their country, cannot approach a political canvass like the present without appreciating keenly the real issues of the contest. It will not be amiss, however, for me to say that I join you in the belief that Gen. Grant has been a gallant soldier [immense applause and cheers] ; that he has done a service to his country in the field which cannot be over-estimated [applause] ; that he has conducted the affairs of the Government, since he has been Chief Magistrate, with great discretion and integrity, and has shown himself in every way disposed to peace at home and abroad, and entirely free from personal self-seeking and aggrandizement. [Applause.] We are here to express to the country our continued confidence in Gen. Grant and our purpose to elect him as President for a second term. [Uproarious applause, shouts and cheers—the audience rising, and many waving their hats.] And we are fortunate in having associated with him a man who has always been our staunch friend, and has, as a legislator, shown the greatest wisdom and integrity. [Applause.]

I am quite sure that we will not make ourselves misunderstood to-day by expressing any ill-feeling towards our late enemies in the field, because we have no such ill-feeling. We know that the hatchet is buried, and we are disposed to do all in our power to co-operate with people in all sections of our land in forwarding the prosperity of our country. But for rulers, comrades, let us select men who in the hour of their country's peril were true. [Applause.] Let us, of all things, refuse our support to men who believed that there was right in secession! [Shouts of applause.]

And now, comrades of Pennsylvania, I desire to express to you a hope that comes from my heart. Gen. Hartranft [enthusiastic applause], your candidate for Governor, is my old comrade and tried friend. [Applause.] He went into the field with us at the first battle of the war, and joined the North Carolina expedition at Annapolis. From that time until the end of the war we were together; on the fields of Roanoke, Newberne, South Mountain, Antietam, Fredericksburg, Vicksburg, Knoxville, Campbell's Station, Blue Spring, the Rapidan campaign from the Wilderness to Appomattox Court-House [applause], he proved himself an efficient and gallant soldier. Comrades of Pennsylvania, it is clearly your duty, without reference to politics, to see that so gallant and true a comrade is not harmed by the malicious slanders of designing politicians. [Three immense cheers were here given for Gen. Hartranft.] You have but for a moment to think of the course pursued during the war by his opponent, Mr. Buckalew, in order to find the strongest reason for the firm support of Hartranft. [Applause.]

Comrades, my personal duties require me to leave you before the deliberations of your meeting are concluded. As you all know, I am engaged in civil pursuits; I have never in my life solicited an office, and never expect to. I can therefore speak to you my unbiased sentiments. I beg of you to make every honest effort to re-elect Gen. Grant, and to elect Gen. Hartranft to the office of Governor of the great Commonwealth of Pennsylvania. [Renewed shouts of applause, and cheers.]

It gives me great pleasure, comrades, to announce to you that the National Committee proposes to you as your temporary chairman, our gallant comrade, so well known to every soldier in the land, Gen. Joseph R. Hawley, of Connecticut. [Loud and prolonged cheering.]

Gen. Hawley's name was greeted with loud and continued applause, and as he appeared on the platform the cheering was again renewed. He spoke as follows :—

GENERAL HAWLEY'S SPEECH.

Gen. Joseph R. Hawley, of Connecticut, was then chosen temporary chairman, and came forward, when he was greeted with "Three cheers for Gen. Hawley," which were given with a will. He then said :—

COMRADES AND FELLOW-CITIZENS—I judge, from the aspect of the great city—from the multitudes that throng its streets, and the continuous roll of drums and these great cheers, that a certain statesman of the land is slightly mistaken. The time for the soldier has come. [Applause.] The time for the soldier is now, and always will be in this land [cries of "That's so"], not to be called to the battle-field, I trust, perhaps, never again. I hope this may always be the land of peace, and there will always be occasion here for hat spirit of patriotism and self-sacrificing loyalty to the country—that devoted attachment to republican principles, that love of order, and civil law, and peace, that distinguishes the American soldier—the *spirit* of the army, that we are thinking of, not the army *organization*. This distinguished statesman has told us the time for the soldier has passed.

I think, judging by the slanders and these malignant attacks on General Grant, that the spirit of the rebellion is still rife. They say that the doctrine of secession is now at rest, and that the policy of the nation is unduly severe and harsh towards the men who were engaged in the late rebellion—that the time for the soldier to appear as a patriot and voter has come again. We have heard "that the pen is mightier than the sword;" so it is in the long run. Charles Sumner has been an eloquent and powerful advocate of the principles over which this great contest was fought. The sword was merely used as a last resort in deciding this contest of ideas.

Half a generation has passed over our heads in discussing this question. The contest was as fierce in the Senate-chamber and on the field of politics as it was on the battle-field.

Now, then, to remove the presence of the soldier is an offense to those who were defeated. What shall we say in the presence of his assertion, and in the presence of an orator who is no less distinguished for his part in the Grant campaign, and loose men who are crying and lamenting, as Horace Greeley laments, in his letter of acceptance to the Baltimore Convention, and that where the spirit of rebellion is unable to send to places of trust—Palmer, Davis, Breckenridge, every man of them rebels.

This same Horace Greeley is the man who desires Jefferson Davis and Breckenridge to be returned to the U. S. Senate. I want to know which is the greatest offense, the presence of Grant or Sumner? To have a regimental flag, with its inscription, is out of place, as Sumner says. If it be out of place, then Grant is the flag bearing the odious inscription; then, if we have to remove Grant, then let us remove Sumner and his ten volumes of orations; also you must level every grave. That will furnish a reminder of their vanquished enemy. This is what Sumner speaks to us: You must remove every monument of the old contest.

These men who, ten years ago, went to the front and periled their lives in the defense of the country, are to be told, it is said, to take back seats—go to the rear, lest, indeed, their presence may be offensive to those who were loyal in the rebellion. Of all the charges that this combination make against us, none is to me more offensive than that—that we are actuated by some spirit of hate and by a policy of revenge. Now, we may safely say, that we challenge the history of any country to produce such a record as ours—such a record of magnanimity expressed by this Union.

Wherever we went in the South we fed the women and children whose husbands and brothers were engaged in rebellion against the Government.

I remember well a little chapter in my own experience in Wilmington, North Carolina, of receiving ten thousand men from Andersonville, whom we fed, and also fed seven thousand white women, a majority of whom had relations in the rebellion. Was that the spirit of hate, or the policy of revenge? And when the last day of the contest came, and General Grant went modestly under the apple-tree at Appomattox and conducted the services of surrender, what did this nation, through its chosen chief soldier, do?—this nation that had sacrificed five thousand millions of dollars and half a million of lives—this Union that then had within its grasp the last of the rebellion—what did it do? What did it say to those men? It let them go to their homes, not to be molested by the United States authorities so long as they obeyed the laws. Was that the spirit of hate? [Cheers]. Was that the spirit of revenge? [Cries of "No! no!"] And the great soldier of the land said this to the civilians of the land. Many of them were clamorous for revenge, and men reproached him, and rebuked him for his excessive clemency.

After the papers were signed, General Lee turned to General Grant and said: "General Grant, there is one thing I had forgotten; the papers are signed; it is, perhaps, too late now; it is this: I was about to observe that many of our men in the ranks own their horses, both in the artillery and cavalry. I would ask that they might have them, as you have permitted the officers to take their side-arms."

"No matter about the papers," said General Grant; "I will give orders to the officers to let these men take their horses home with them; they will need them in the spring ploughing." [Cheers.]

There was a great army, victorious and triumphant, the army of the United States, and these men would have us believe that our spirit was the same then as it is to-day, and the same to-day as it was then: that they are animated by a spirit of hatred and revenge; was this saying to these men who were engaged in the war, go home, rest at peace, just obey the laws, and take your horses home with you, and feeding them too, the men dividing their haversacks with them [cheers], and that too by the thousands—these same rebel soldiers had been taught to hate the Yankees, but this act caused the tears to pour down their cheeks. This was an inexpressible magnanimity. Was this a policy of hate or revenge? No; we are the same to-day as then. Did we confiscate property? No. Did we banish them? Never a man of them. Several thousand of them felt a bitter hatred to the old flag, and swore they would never live under its folds. They banished themselves to South America. In a short time many of these men were hungry, ragged, and home-sick, and Uncle Sam brought them home free by the hundreds. Was this, again, the policy of hate or revenge?

Yes, comrades, this was our government. This was our Republican party governing the Union then; and, when a grievous visitation of Providence brought starvation to the South, our Congress, by our own free will, voted, one session, five millions of dollars to feed them. The purses of the North were opened, and the granaries discharged of their benefits. This, indeed, was not the policy of hate and of revenge.

We have one request indeed to make of these men. We have but one disability, one link of approval remaining. Only one statute remains—one act of legislation to show the sense of this nation that this great rebellion was a crime. That is the temporary seclusion from office of a few, a very few of the guilty superiors, the terribly guilty leaders who dragged their people into this awful slaughter. We say to some of them—less than three hundred remain now—you cannot hold office again until Congress permits. We have one thing to say to these men. We had, at the close of the war, really but one thing to ask of them. Every step of reconstructed legislation, every act taken by the Republican Congress, every act, and every order of General Grant, has had in view this—the safety of the lives and the persons and the property of our loyal brothers at the South.

We have confiscated no property and banished nobody. We whipped no one, drowned no one, we have hanged no one. Gentlemen, men who were in the rebellion, can you say as much for yourselves since the war? [Cries of "No, no."] Have you done none of these things to our friends down there? If we have ever been angry, it is these which have filled us with righteous indignation after the flag marched in triumph over every foot of Southern soil—after you have professed to have surrendered in good faith, and to have accepted the situation. Week after week, and month after month the cry came up, and was from many of the white regions in the South, that the loyal white men and the poor black men were taken from their homes—were scourged—were sometimes drowned, sometimes banished, sometimes hanged—that they could not enjoy their homes or raise their crops in peace; that they could not hold Republican meetings, or any meetings in honor of the flag. This has been the complaint from mouth to mouth and year to year. If we have some harshness in our legislation, it was that this might be prevented. Why, in the name of God and humanity, was this just and fair to these men, and why do they come to us with the pretense of shaking hands across the bloodier chasm, when there is a chasm and a bloody chasm at their own door—a chasm of their own making, which we shall have to bridge over. Do that first, and you will find the great heart of the North, where it has been aching to have all men praying for the day when justice and peace may prevail every-where; and the answer to all the appeals of these men, in answer to all their cries, I have but one thing to say, I would placard it upon all cross-roads. I would put it upon every court-house. I would print it upon every door in the South. I would have it where every one might read it: "Do unto others as you would have others do unto you." [Great cheers.]

I say I shall not think of eulogizing here Ulysses S. Grant before these soldiers. [Cheers.] There is not an audience in this land that needs it less. There are people, however, that ought to be reminded of what he has done for the country. [Laughter.] There are men who are famous as defenders of the land, whose speeches are daily filled, and papers whose columns are crowded with defamation of the man.

They look in at the back door of his house, they peep into his cellar, they smell about his stables, they hunt for the title-deeds of his lands, they search through the certificates of stock that he may hold, they suffer no relation of life to be met without putting upon it the venomous stain of their slander. There never has been a presidential candidate, since the organization of the Government, so venomously, unceasingly, and unforgivingly pursued. I beg for him, in the name of the memories of the past—I beg for General Grant something of that universal amnesty of which they are talking. [Cheers.] Forgive him! Forgive him! [Cheers and laughter.] He may sometimes have erred. He may have made a mis-take. He may not be absolutely beautiful or sublimely perfect. [Laughter.] There never was but one man who was perfect. General Grant may have erred sometimes in the appoint-ments he has made. Alas! I know that the cry of his enemies is that he did make many mistakes; but I say we can afford to overlook some things, and we must remind these men of some things also that he has done for the land. They say he is a man of no capacity.

There are several thousands of us who started early in the war as captains and as colonels. One of them went up and up and up; and again, by the unanimous cry of his party, he was sent up again until he was called to Washington, and the little man, as he gave him his commission said: "Take this; as the people now trust you, so under God they will sustain you," and then every loyal heart in this land prayed God that this little man, who seemed to have been brought from obscurity to save us and to lead us to triumph, would succeed; and when he went down to the Wilderness we knew there was fighting to be done. Then, my comrades, you of the Western armies know that there was a soldier over the army of the Potomac and that there was a man at the head who meant work. [Cries of "Good" and cheers.] There was a little man who meant victory, and we all knew that if ever this country was to be saved it was to be saved in those months. On the first, second, and third of May, 1864, we hastily perfected our muster-rolls, we gathered our clothing and provisions, and sent back our surplus baggage. We hurried off the long roll. How many gallant boys heard their names called for the last time that night. Next morning all along the great circle we started forward and fought in the Wilderness, over miles of broken land, where a man could no more than see his comrade. We were slaughtered that day, and the next day, and the next. The fourth day and the fifth we fought until the darkness fell upon us. They did not know what we were doing or what we might do. Able men came to Grant and said: "General, we must stop a day or two. We must indeed bury these dead men; we must, indeed; really, we cannot go on. We need more clothing. We must halt." Said the great general, "You have done very well so far—very well under all the circumstances. To-morrow morning at half-past three the army goes forward" [great cheering]; and, terrible as the slaughter was, as you answer now to the memory of it, so the great heart of the nation answered, "Go on," and on the night of the sixth day he wrote a little dispatch: "Our losses have been severe; we have captured Johnson's division and two brigades besides, and we have taken about thirty pieces of artillery, and it seems to be with us. I shall fight it out on this line, if it takes all summer." [Renewed cheering.]

I wonder if all these enemies of Grant remember how they felt in those days—followed him through the Wilderness to the Appomattox, of which we have spoken. As a soldier he was everything the crisis demanded; as a victor, after dictating terms never equaled for magnanimity, instead of affording him triumph or even time to rest, he started right from Richmond, and took his bag and started for Washington. [Cheers.] He started for Washington, and telegraphed to stop expenses; and whatever his course has been, it has been marked throughout with forbearance; whatever has been done has been done for peace, life, and prosperity throughout the land. Now, a single word and I am done. [Cries of "Go on."] The election of a candidate in the field against General Grant would have several meanings. I give as the first of them, it would be the triumph of a man who believes in the theoretical meaning of secession. Now, I appeal to the files of the *Tribune* for the winter of 1860 and 1861, for the countless declarations to that effect. They are known to the people of the land. [A voice. "And the year '63 also."] You are right; all along through the war. And if it be said that these declarations of the newspaper press may not be directly authorized by him; if it be said these were the sentiments then entertained, and since laid aside, I appeal to the history of the "American Conflict," written since the great struggle was over—deliberately in review of the principles and acts of the great struggle—many years back; in the first volume, on the 39th page of the book, if I remember rightly, he says in substance: "If any considerable number of States desire to go out, let them go, and I would resist all measures devised to keep them in by force." [Cries of "Never," and hisses.] This was the sentiment of Horace Greeley; and with a full knowledge of what I am saying—and I feel the consciousness of the presence here, and I am fully aware of these busy pens and wires—I say to you here, that whatever there be left of the spirit of rebellion in this land to-day, these are the sentiments of Horace Greeley; and if he be elected, there will be a man in the presidential chair entertaining in substance the sentiments of James Buchanan; and with these declarations in view, in the event of another insurrection, Horace Greeley would say the same thing as James Buchanan. It is impossible to see how we could call upon him at the first symptom of insurrection to put it down. It has another significance now. We may differ about the details of amnesty. We are all well agreed in this, that if entire perfect peace and justice would really and thoroughly be established in the South, it would bring very soon an entire amnesty. And we are also perfectly aware that the day has not come for that state of affairs. Horace Greeley, by his letter of acceptance addressed to the Baltimore Convention, dwells at some length upon the harshness of forbidding the people of the South to choose its men to rule over them—there being only three hundred so excluded. According to Horace Greeley, there is a desire to elect these three hundred with Jeff. Davis at their head. He stands as the peculiar representative of that sentiment, and the election of Horace Greeley will be to say that we are willing for those men to come back to places of power. [Cries of " No, no."]

Thirdly, the elevation of Horace Greeley would mean this, that the nation has been unduly harsh and unjustly severe in dealing with the rebels. That is one of the greatest points, perhaps the chief point made by them against us. If we are unduly harsh and unjustly severe in dealing with the rebellion, it is not the Republican party alone, but the nation; for the policy of the Union has been, during those eleven years, not to confiscate or take away their property; they have not hanged a man or tried a man for treason. Has this great nation been severe in dealing with them? Is that the judgment of the past eleven years? The nation is asked as a jury to send in a verdict that this party is tried, and is found too cruel to continue in power. Will the people of this country give that verdict? [Cries of "No, no."]

But further: there is one other point that the success of our enemies would decide. One other paragraph in the verdict of the elevation of Greeley would be to say that General Grant is found personally unworthy of his high position. Is not that so? Do not all their writers and their presses dwell largely, to the exclusion, I might say, of other things, upon the personal unfitness and personal unworthiness of General Grant? Then the triumph of our opponents would be the decision of these few points.

Now, gentlemen, it is entirely competent and proper for us, who have been soldiers, to have soldiers rule over the American people. We are not seeking to inaugurate a civil war, and we are not seeking to inaugurate a policy of hate and revenge; but we have come here to ask for those rights for which our brothers died, and that they shall not be periled by the wiles of scheming and corrupt politicians. Now, I have entertained you too long already, and we will proceed to the deliberations of the Convention.

Three cheers were proposed for General Hawley, and given with a will.

CALL OF THE CONVENTION.

At the conclusion of General Hawley's address the call for the Convention was read by Col. James Corcoran, of Williamsport, Pa., the temporary Secretary of the Convention. After the reading of the call, Col. L. E. Dudley, Secretary of the Veterans' National Committee, presented to the Convention a huge roll of manuscript, which he partially unrolled. Col. Dudley was greeted with cheers, in recognition of the services he has rendered in organizing the Convention. He spoke as follows:—

REMARKS OF COLONEL DUDLEY.

COMRADES—As Secretary of the Veterans' National Committee, I desire to present a roll of signatures of our comrades throughout the country who have approved the call which has just been read. The roll is at least six hundred feet long, containing upwards of fifty thousand names. I hope, Mr. Chairman, as I am very hoarse, that you will excuse me from reading the names. [Laughter and applause.]

TEMPORARY ORGANIZATION.

The States and Territories were then called, and each delegation named one person to act as temporary Vice-President and one as Secretary. The list, when completed, was as follows:—

New Hampshire—S. L. Guff, V. P.; Maj. E. Vaughn, Sec.
Massachusetts—Capt. D. G. McNamara, V. P.; Lieut. O. Chamberlain, Sec.
Connecticut—Lieut. F. M. Welsh, V. P.; Sergt. E. A. Perry, Sec.
New Jersey—Col. A. Way, V. P.; J. G. Ogden, Sec.
Pennsylvania—Col. Wm. McMichael, V. P.; Col. J. Cochrane, Sec.
Ohio—Capt. P. G. Watmough, V. P.; A. A. Graham, Sec.
Indiana—Gen. R. Williams, V. P.; Sergt. A. Sabine, Sec.
Iowa—Col. H. R. Stewart, V. P.; J. R. Hammond, Sec.
Michigan—Gen. W. A. Throop, V. P.; Gen. F. M. Swift, Sec.
Wisconsin—Capt. H. W. Walbridge, V. P.; Capt. T. Kay, Sec.
Illinois—E. J. Rook, V. P.; Gen. D. E. N. Magee, Sec.
Mississippi—C. E. Pierce, V. P.; S. B. Sturtevant, Sec.
Kansas—Maj. J. C. Wilkinsham, V. P.; R. J. Brown, Sec.

California—Capt. Hartmyer, V. P.; W H. Lowrie, Sec.
Delaware—Capt. N. Bayne, V. P.; Capt. E. C. Stakenburg, Sec.
Maryland—Col. W. H. Soudermilk, V. P.; Capt. J. R. Kinney, Sec.
Virginia—Maj. E. E. White, V. P.; Maj. C. C. Miller, Sec.
North Carolina—Sergt. G. L. Mobson, V. P.
Georgia—Col. G. J. Taggart, V. P.; Capt. F. Hillgart, Sec.
Alabama—Gen. J. W. Burke, V. P.; Capt. G. H. Patrick, Sec.
Florida—Gen. C. M. Hamilton, V. P.
Kentucky—Gen. S. N. Price, V. P.; Col. C. P. Willcox, Sec.
Mississippi—J. C. Tucker, V. P.; C. W. Clark, Sec.
Louisiana—Sergt. C. P. Darrell, V. P.; Capt. W. H. Wharton, Sec.
Texas—Gen. A. G. Maloy, V. P.; Capt. T. D. Mitchell, Sec.
West Virginia—Gen. H. Duvall, V. P.; Capt. C. J. Rawlins, Sec.
Rhode Island—Col. John McCalmut. V. P.; Gen. K. M. Hoyt, Sec.
South Carolina—Maj. R. H. Willoughby, V. P.; Capt. N. K. Reed, Sec.

THE FLAG OF FORD'S THEATRE.

General Hawley here arose and called the attention of the Convention to a large silk flag hanging from one of the upper private boxes, of which he said: " You will remember, when Abraham Lincoln was assassinated there hung above the stage-box in which he sat a large flag, which vindicated itself and became the means by which the assassin was finally brought to merited punishment."

LETTER FROM PRESIDENT GRANT.

The following letter was then read to the Convention. When the Secretary had finished reading it, long and continued cheers were given for the writer.

LONG BRANCH, N. J., Sept. 9, 1872.

COL. L. E. DUDLEY, *Secretary Veterans' National Committee:*
Dear Sir—I am in receipt of your letter of the 4th inst., extending to me, by your committee, a pressing invitation to attend the grand Mass Convention of Veteran Soldiers, to be held in the city of Pittsburg on the 17th inst.
My desire to attend, and meet again so many old companions in arms, is very great, but my judgment tells me to leave the celebration entirely to those whose motives cannot be misunderstood. I know of no class of citizens better entitled to meet in convention and to have weight accorded to their views on all national matters there expressed, than the veteran soldiers who risked their lives for the honor and perpetuity of their country. I am sure your councils will be marked by wisdom and patriotism, and that the meeting of so many comrades will be a joyous and an advantageous one. I wish for you all that you expect from your meeting of the 17th inst., and only regret that I cannot be with you on that occasion.

With great respect, your obedient servant,
U. S. GRANT.

At half-past one, P. M., the Convention adjourned, to meet again at three o'clock.

AFTERNOON SESSION.

At three o'clock General Hawley called the Convention to order. A choir, composed of one hundred gentlemen and ladies, on the stage, led by Prof. William Pope, sang the " Battle-cry of Freedom," accompanied by Conner's band, of New York, the whole audience joining in the chorus. General Hawley, waving his handkerchief, kept time, and the inspiring strains thrilled every heart in the immense audience. At the close three loud and long cheers were given, as much in appreciation of the music as in thanks to the musicians.

During the interval which was necessitated by the correction of lists of temporary officers, Major Willard Bullard, of New York, read the following letter from General Daniel E. Sickles. The name of General Sickles was greeted with the warmest enthusiasm, as also the names of Generals Hawley, Burnside, and Logan, who rose and bowed in acknowledgment of the honor done them:—

LETTER OF GENERAL SICKLES.

MADRID, Saturday, August 24, 1872.

COMRADES—Official duties far away from home prevent my acceptance of the invitation to address your meeting.

You, who have sustained by your vote and voice the noble cause for which you fought, have been told you must congratulate yourselves when you see the capitulation of Appomattox in '65 followed by the surrender at Baltimore in '72. You have noticed some suspicious tactics about that surrender. At the moment when the enemy drop their flag and adopt yours, they advance to the attack. This is an old trick often tried in the war. The Democrats say they have adopted Republican principles and Republican candidates, but they mean to destroy the Republican party. They admire your camp, but they modestly think they are worthier than you to occupy it.

You are told that you must again reach across the bloody chasm and shake hands with the other side. You have done it already. Everybody is forgiven who has asked forgiveness. The unrepentant few who stand out defy the judgment of their country and of mankind. Let them wait. Neither honor nor duty demand more than has been magnanimously given to those who contrived the ruin and disgrace of their country. Mr. Greeley argues that we must open the doors of the White House to Jeff. Davis before we can have peace. If this is what is meant by "reconciliation," it seems to me that Mr. Greeley and Mr. Sumner wasted breath in resisting the policy of Andrew Johnson, and owe that persecuted gentleman a penitential pilgrimage to his retreat in Tennessee.

Gen. Schurz tells us Grant is too much of a soldier to be a good president. Such, I am persuaded, is not the public judgment. Gen. Schurz should study his logic before bringing such an argument to Republicans, for he helped to elect Grant in '68. Nor can it have weight with Democrats, since they all supported McClellan in '64. Ask Illinois if Logan is less worthy of her trust because he led an army corps in the West. Ask Wisconsin if Fairchild failed as her Governor because he bore her flag in battle. Ask Maine if she regrets the honors bestowed on Chamberlain. Ask Connecticut if she admires Hawley more in the field than in council. Ask Rhode Island whether her chivalrous Burnside made a bad Governor because he was a good soldier.

Governor Fenton leaves the Republican party because he desires to purify the National Government. You can estimate his sincerity and success when you see that he has secured for his enterprise the aid of Tammany Hall! Our people do not sacrifice their convictions to leaders, no matter how eminent. Soldiers will not desert Grant to follow Schurz! The colored people will not follow even Sumner to Jeff. Davis! Reformers will not follow Fenton to Tammany Hall!

It is difficult to understand Mr. Greeley's platform of "reconciliation," which consists in abandoning his old friends to embrace his old enemies. Nor is it easy to accept Mr. Sumner's new revelation of peace, which denounces "a policy of hate" in terms of passionate resentment against the President and his supporters.

Mr. Greeley, as the Democratic candidate for the Presidency, hails his new supporters as the best Republicans he has ever seen. If the Republican Convention at Philadelphia had nominated Horatio Seymour, it may be presumed he would have found that body more democratic than the Democratic Convention at Baltimore.

Mr. Greeley, although gifted with remarkable talents, is not fit for the Presidency. As a member of Congress and of the convention called to amend the Constitution of New York —the principal public employments he has filled—Mr. Greeley failed to equal the expectations suggested by his success as a journalist. Powerful as an agitator, it is precisely in the qualities necessary for the direction of affairs that Mr. Greeley has shown no aptitude. As a leader he lacks tenacity of purpose, and at critical moments he is deficient in fortitude. For example: In 1861, when the South determined to fight for slavery, Mr. Greeley, who had done as much as anybody to precipitate the conflict, advised acquiescence when the rebels, with arms in their hands, demanded separation from the Union. In 1864, when our cause more than ever needed firmness in council and vigor in action, Mr. Greeley, dismayed and demoralized by the difficulties of the situation, advised—nay, insisted, with all the authority of his position, that President Lincoln should negotiate with the enemy. At that juncture his advice was like that given in the platform adopted by the Northern Democrats, in the same year, at Chicago— with the difference that, while they had consistently opposed the war in all its stages, Mr. Greeley vibrated between impatient demands for the prosecution of hostilities and discouraging appeals to accept a discreditable peace.

And now, after sustaining all the reconstruction measures of the Republican party, after pressing Congress to enact laws to protect the rights of the enfranchised freedmen, he changes front, and, adopting the old State Rights dogma of the Democratic party, maintains that all guaranties for personal rights must be sought exclusively in the State Governments. To these indications of a volatile character, without adhesiveness to convictions, might be added various proofs of his present indifference to objects that, sixty days ago, he professed to believe of prime importance—such, for instance, as the maintenance of a protective tariff and the ascendency of the Republican party—the political organization and the one measure of political economy with which he has been heretofore consistently identified.

These latter tergiversations unhappily coincide with his nomination for the Presidency by a party which he had for many years opposed with notable vehemence. Whether such incidents point to weakness of purpose or the temptations of ambition, or whether, as may be more leniently supposed, the Republican party has outlived Mr. Greeley's liking for it, are matters about which there is much speculation. It is enough to affirm that Mr. Greeley's attitude as a candidate, regarded either as a stratagem to gain power, or as a sudden conversion to new opinions, shows him to be unworthy of the support of any Republican and unworthy of the confidence of any Democrat.

The new institutions of the Republic are only safe while guarded by the great party that created them. Until the tardy acquiescence of the Democratic party in the letter of these enactments shall be followed by their voluntary incorporation in the legislation of the States controlled by Mr. Greeley's new friends, it is impossible to separate the issues of the day from the issues of the war. The re-election of Gen. Grant is as essential to establish the Government on the sure foundations of the amended Constitution, as the re-election of Mr. Lincoln was necessary to the preservation of the Union. We have given immunity for the past—we must have security for the future.

If the Democratic Legislatures of Kentucky, Maryland, and Delaware had passed Mr. Sumner's Civil Rights bill; if the last Democratic Legislature of New York had not endeavored impotently to recall the assent given by their Republican predecessors to the Fifteenth Amendment to the Constitution; if the Democratic members of the House of Representatives had not refused again and again to sanction the laws passed by Congress to execute the late amendments to the Federal Constitution, it might not demand excessive credulity to believe the recent action of the Baltimore Convention to be something else than a shallow electioneering contrivance.

As it is, we must believe that, as the rebel armies surrendered when further resistance was impossible, and not until then, so the Democrats nominated Mr. Greeley because they had lost all hope of defeating Gen. Grant by any choice they could make from their own ranks. Both the convention and the candidate have exhibited unusual facility of adaptation to their new situation. They unite in a reciprocal amnesty for the past, from which only Gen. Grant and the Republican party are excluded. They pledge an irrevocable fellowship for the future, which depends on no other contingency than their success in ascertaining whether the Democrats became Republicans when they nominated Mr. Greeley, or whether Mr. Greeley became a Democrat when he accepted their nomination.

Comrades! you saw the same coalition and heard the same appeals in 1866, when President Johnson "swung around the circle." Mr. Seward once gave to a similar movement the sanction of his great name. In 1868 Justice Chase was a candidate for Democratic favor on the same plan of operations. The most successful column always loses a few stragglers. The Republican party survived the desertion of Johnson, the hostility of Seward, and the conversion of Chase. The campaigns of 1866 and 1868 were not seriously affected by any of these casualties, because the measures of the Republican party satisfied the country. It remains to be seen whether Mr. Greeley, Mr. Sumner, Mr. Trumbull, and Mr. Fenton exercise the control over public opinion which is claimed for them.

No Republican can fairly complain that Gen. Grant has not adhered faithfully to the principles asserted by that organization. In his great office he has shown judgment, firmness, and moderation. Indifferent to the exaggeration and detraction always heard in the discussions of any excited canvass, the "sober second thought" of the people will prove that they are neither ungrateful nor unjust in their appreciation of a great soldier and a wise ruler. Grant has never lost a battle nor betrayed a cause. Let us follow him once more to victory!

Faithfully yours,

D. E. SICKLES.

Col. L. E. Dudley, *Secretary Veterans' National Committee, New York.*

FROM THE SOLDIERS' HOME, DAYTON, OHIO.

The following telegram of greeting was also read :—

DAYTON, OHIO, Sept. 17, 1872.

GEN. A. E. BURNSIDE, *National Soldiers' and Sailors' Convention :*

The Union Soldiers of the National Asylum send greetings to their comrades assembled God grant you may have prosperity, unanimity, and victory.

C. H. FERNOLD,
President Grant and Wilson Club, National Soldiers' Home.

LETTER FROM SCHUYLER COLFAX.

The following letter from Schuyler Colfax was received with cheers :—

SOUTH BEND, IND., September 13, 1872.

My Dear Mr. Dudley—I appreciate highly the honor of your invitation to the Soldiers' and Sailors' Convention at Pittsburg on the 17th inst., but regret that I cannot be present, having promised to be in Northern Michigan with my family at that time. In the dark days, when the unity and nationality of the Republic were imperiled, they were at the perilous front. In these brighter days of peace, it is but fitting that they should have front seats, and realize also the justice and gratitude of their countrymen.

Yours truly,
SCHUYLER COLFAX.

To COL. L. E. DUDLEY, Secretary, etc.

LETTER FROM GENERAL SIGEL.

The following letter was greeted with great enthusiasm by the Convention :—

NEW YORK, September 13, 1872.

COL. L. E. DUDLEY, *Secretary Soldiers' and Sailors' National Committee :*

Dear Sir—Your kind letter inviting me to be present at the Soldiers' and Sailors' Convention at Pittsburg on the 17th inst., is received. I remember with pride and pleasure the first great convention held in that same city, in September, 1866, when resolutions were passed indorsing the policy of Congress, and especially the passage of the Fourteenth Amendment by that body. At that time there was no doubt in our mind that certain constitutional guaranties were necessary to prevent reaction, define American citizenship, and create a uniform system of national representation throughout the Republic.

The work of the Convention was good and noble, but it is a remarkable fact that only in 1868, two years afterward, the Fourteenth Amendment was ratified, while it took two years more (March 30, 1870) before the Fifteenth Amendment, in regard to universal suffrage, was finally adopted.

There was one fierce and continuous political struggle for more than five years after the war was closed—in Congress, in the press, on the stump, and in every nook and corner of the land—surpassing in its earnestness and grandeur even the great debates of the French Revolution, when the "rights of man" were discussed and declared. Of course, before the new basis of the future life of the Union was established, there was not and could not be peace and harmony between the North and South. This, at least, was the opinion of those very men who now go back on their own acts by disavowing as tyrannical and unnecessary the very means without which no such basis would exist at the present time. It anything is absurd, it is this absurdity of accusing and defaming the executive instruments of their own self-divined plans and purposes, and to curse the children of their own love. If anything is unjust, it is the endeavor to take a man to account for official acts which were forced upon him by Congressional legislation, inasmuch as political ostracism and military rule in the South after the war were neither proposed nor inaugurated by General Grant. If there is treachery, it is this indirect appeal to the South to revolt against the past policy of the Government, on which to-day rest the unity, the security, and liberty of the Republic!

As in 1861, so we are now again on the defensive—not against a formidable enemy in the field, but against a coalition which we distrust, as it is influenced by ambition and disappointment, and tends to the revival of questions which we regarded as settled. Under the profession of reconciliation, amnesty, and reform, with nothing to stand upon except nicely framed platforms and pronunciamentos, this strange alliance of Guelphs and Ghibellines tries to put its double-faced policy into practice. We cannot trust mere professions. We cannot intrust ourselves to a house divided against itself and built on sand. We cannot intrust the most sacred rights, interests, and liberties of the American people to a coalition which is not based on real facts and deeds, and above all suspicion and apprehension, to undo, or change, or cripple what was attained by a terrible struggle, and paid for by the best blood of our people and milliards of dollars.

For these reasons, and others of secondary consideration, I cannot be in favor of the Cincinnati nominees, but shall stand with you on the side of Grant and Wilson.

But, while I am in their favor, I hope to see in their election not a mere personal or temporary triumph. I hope that abuses, where they exist, will be abolished; perfect harmony between the North and South restored by wise measures of conciliation and material support; that civil service reform will be extended and perfected by recognizing the right of the whole people, without difference of party, to be represented in the administration of offices, and that the soldiers and sailors of the Union will be, as they have always been, the most zealous and faithful supporters of our civil government, the Constitution and laws of the American Republic.

Very respectfully and truly yours,

F. SIGEL.

A GREETING TO PRESIDENT GRANT.

A delegate now moved that the fifty thousand soldiers here assembled in Convention, send a greeting to General Ulysses S. Grant, President, with the assurance that they will give him their united support in November. .

The motion was adopted amid thunders of applause.

A communication was then read from over seven hundred ex-Confederate soldiers, expressing their preference for General Grant.

At the conclusion of the reading by the Secretary, the choir, accompanied by the band, struck up the grand old battle-hymn of the Republic, "John Brown," the whole audience rising and joining in the chorus. When silence was secured, General Hartranft was escorted to the front of the stage, and, in response to the wildest and most unbounded enthusiasm, said:—

REMARKS OF GENERAL HARTRANFT.

COMRADES—I thank you for this demonstration, not for myself, but for the Republican cause. [Cheers.] It is no more credit to me than, when we were fighting in the front. and regiment after regiment was going forward, you kept your eye upon the colors. [Cheers.] Not upon the man who carried them; because, when he fell, another took his place. So in this contest keep your eye well on the colors, and we will win *this* contest as we have ever done in the field. [Cheers.]

The enthusiasm which followed General Hartranft's brief remarks was so unusually prolonged that General Hawley, the Chairman, after several endeavors, could only secure quiet by the familiar command, "Attention, battalion!" which elicited renewed cheers and laughter. When silence was secured, General Hawley said:—

The Committee on Permanent Organization is ready to report.

REPORT OF COMMITTEE ON PERMANENT ORGANIZATION.

General Baker, of Minnesota, from the Committee on Permanent Organization, then said:—

"In the absence of our chairman, General Rutherford, I have the honor to report that our choice for Permanent Chairman of this Convention is General John A. Logan, of Illinois. [Cheers.]

The action of the committee was unanimously ratified by the Convention rising and cheering loud and long.

General Stuart L. Woodford, of New York, Captain A. T. Maupin, of Virginia, and

Private J. T. Purnell, of Pennsylvania, were selected as a committee to escort the President-elect to the chair, now vacated by General Hawley. General Logan was received with enthusiastic and prolonged cheering. He said :—

SPEECH OF GENERAL LOGAN.

FELLOW COMRADES—I feel very highly complimented indeed, in being chosen to preside over the deliberations of a body of men composed of veterans who have done so much for their country as has been done by yourselves, in connection with your associates, in the late war. If there is any people in this land who have a right to meet together, consult together, and determine one with another as to the course they shall pursue in reference to political matters, it does seem to me that the veteran soldiers of this country are those people. You have not met together, my comrades, as has been said by our enemies, for the purpose of exciting feelings in your breast against those in opposition to you politically—not for the purpose of making the breach wider and wider between ourselves and our enemies—not for the purpose of causing the bloody chasm, as it is denominated, to grow wider and deeper, but for the purpose of consulting together as to what is best to be done in order to preserve the great fruits of your labors, and the labors of the loyal people of this land. [Prolonged applause.]

Our country was said, prior to the late rebellion, to be free—to be the free home of the people of all climes who desire to reside with us. But, until your action produced certain results that were produced recently, until that freedom that is now enjoyed by all was brought on by a strong arm, it was not a free land. But to-day, thank God, the same right that you have to meet together and decide as to your course politically, or to take some action in regard to the affairs of this great nation—that same right belongs to every man, black, white, or of any complexion, or of any race, whatever it may be, who are or may be dwelling within the confines of the United States of America. [Applause.] This country, then, is a free land to all men; and not only that, my countrymen and fellow-soldiers, but is to-day the proudest in every respect. It presents to-day an aspect of civilization, of refinement, of progress, that is presented by no other country in the civilized world. This progress has been going on since 1860, when the power of the Democratic party ceased, and the power of the Republican party commenced—all the progress since that time, and all there is to day that gives a brilliancy to the world, and all that which has been done by the people of this country—I say all of these things are due to you and your associates, veterans, as the loyal people of this country. [Applause.]

Our position, then, to-day, proud as it is, is due to the Republican party. Certainly no man in this land, no matter what his political affiliation may be—there is no man, I presume, but who is proud of the position we occupy to-day. Our position as to relations with foreign countries, with every civilized country, with every country in the world, is one to be proud of. This proud position has been given us by the wise statesmanship and the qualities belonging to the men who are at the head of the party known as the Republican party in this land. [Applause.] It is due to the men now holding the most responsible positions in the country.

I did not intend, nor do I now intend, to detain you [cries of "Go on," "Go on"] in making a political speech of any length, for your work is already accomplished. In calling me to the chair in order to preside over this vast assembly, you only intend me to preside over your deliberations. I repeat here, your work is done, but your speech-making and resolutions will soon follow.

I desire to call the attention of the veterans of this country to the condition of things to-day politically, without denouncing our enemies, which we have no desire to do. We have a friend at the head of the Republican party—the President of the United States of America—U. S. Grant, as our candidate and our standard-bearer. Associated with him is Henry Wilson, of Massachusetts [tremendous applause]—a statesman and an honest man in every sense of the word. Since the time of General Washington and Andrew Jackson, no men have ever been so slandered, so violently abused, as have these men—especially General Grant. I call your attention to the fact that when Washington was President of the United States, after a severe struggle of seven years, at the head of a little army—after he had given liberty to this land—after the people of this land appreciated him as a great statesman and civilian, they made him President of the United States. After he had been President for nearly four years, and when he was a candidate for re-election, some men there were who attacked and maligned him in the same manner as men to-day slander our President. Coming down to Andrew Jackson, who was and is one of the greatest heroes of this land, when he had been President nearly four years, and was again placed in nomination for re-election by a grateful people, a conspiracy was organized in the Senate of the United States for the purpose of destroying his reputation and preventing his re-election. They even entered the sacred precincts of the family altar. The people of this country listened for a time to these slanders—the most vile and shameless, but after a while they said: "We know Jackson. We know that he is an honest man, and know that he is capable of holding the high office he now occupies." So it was, my countrymen, with Jackson, the old hero. But after these slanders had been hurled at him for a time, the people, at the polls, recognized the work of that purest of men, and said, "Again we will make him President of the United States;" and his defamers to-day lie cold and silent, and never a name of one of them is mentioned. The people will always take the man by the hand who is assailed unfairly and dishonestly, as has been the case with the present President of the United States.

My fellow-soldiers, let me say this, that Grant will be elected President of the United States for four years more. [Prolonged applause.] This event will certainly occur. When he passes away from this earth, when he is lying in the cold and silent tomb, he will live not only in the memory of soldiers, but in the history of the United States, in the history of the world, and he will be recognized as one of the greatest sages that has ever lived in this land; and, my fellow-countrymen, when the 5th of November rolls around, and the votes are again counted, if you will pass along the by-ways, alleys, streets, and avenues of our cities, you will find the carcasses of the political hucksters of this land. [Applause.] Carl Schurz was a soldier—I always call a man a soldier that wore the United States uniform; but, as to the other part, whether he was a good soldier or not, I am not his historian, and, therefore, will not judge. I refer his story to Greeley, who gave him a character upon which you can inform yourself at your leisure. When I speak of him I connect him with Trumbull, Tipton, and Sumner. I have nothing to say here to depreciate the ability of all of these men.

But I will say this, that they concluded, when Grant was made President of the United States, on account of their great learning, that they must control this administration. But when they went to Gen. Grant and said, "This must be done, your cabinet must be so, this thing must be done this way," Grant replied, saying, "Gentlemen, I am President of the United States." [Applause.] They found that Grant would select his own cabinet, that Grant would do his own thinking, that he had commanded armies, and Grant was therefore able to attend to the duties of his office too; that he understood why he was placed in that position; when he desired their council, he would ask it. Because they could not use him, they resolved that they would destroy him, and to destroy him they would destroy the Republican party. In destroying the Republican party they would destroy, in my judgment, the peace of mankind. Inside the Republican party lives and dwells the peace and happiness of the people of this land, the hope of freedom, the hope of liberty, of prosperity, of progress, and of everything that makes the country. It was well said by Frederick Douglass, the colored orator, that "The Republican party is the old ship; in it there is life; outside, all is sea and all is death." Now these men conspire against Grant, conspire against the peace, and happiness, and prosperity of this country.

I am sorry that I am compelled to-day to say that some of these men occupy a humiliating position. Schurz boasted that he could control the Germans of this country. In order to alienate the Germans from the present administration, he contends that there was something wrong in the sale of arms to France; but his statements were proven to be untruthful, and what influence does he now exert among the Germans? Charles Sumner, who is from the glorious State of Massachusetts, thought he could control the colored men of this land; and these two men thought, by controlling these two great peoples, they could control the President of the United States. But neither of them have succeeded in getting control of either of these respective parties. Sumner did not write to the citizens of the United States, but he wrote to the colored citizens of the United States, and to his shame be it said —I am sorry that I can say it to-day—he was not able, with all his eloquence and the great name that he has had for many years, even to control the veriest boot-black that belonged to the colored race. [Applause.] It only shows how great men really fail occasionally. He went home to the people of Massachusetts, who stand a solid column in favor of Grant, and that true, honest man, Henry Wilson, from their own State—not having been led astray by Sumner. So far as this mercenary man from St. Louis, Carl Schurz, is concerned, he never uttered a sentiment for Grant unless he was paid for it, and he signally failed to control the German voters of this country. He has failed as signally as has Sumner with the colored voters.

Now, fellow-soldiers of Pennsylvania, let me say but one word for you. You have to-day as gallant a man before you, as your candidate for Governor, as ever bore the standard of this land. [Deafening applause.] He has been assailed in the newspapers and on the stump, for what purpose? For the same purpose that they assailed Gen. Grant and Henry Wilson, and almost every leading man in the Republican party. By assailing Gen. Hartranft, they intend to carry the State of Pennsylvania in your October election against the Republican party, and by carrying it against the Republican party they expect to dampen the ardor of Republicanism everywhere, and in that way gain a victory in the November contest. It was intended for that, and for no other purpose. I was induced to believe, and I do believe to-day, that men claiming to be Republicans, who persistently attack Hartranft, do so for the sake of assisting to make Greeley President of the United States.

Then let me say to you, when you leave this city, where you have received such a hearty welcome, where everything possible has been done for you, where the people here show that they feel that this meeting is for the good of the country, where they say in every possible way they can that their hearts grow great because of Republican institutions—when you go to your homes, go with your hearts full of patriotism, and let it be known that the people everywhere are in favor of your candidate in Pennsylvania. Ah! Pennsylvania has always been called the Keystone State. I feel confident that the Republicans will carry this State. Then let us hear from old Pennsylvania the same old ringing Republican notes that we have ever heard, and we will send back from Illinois, Iowa, Kansas, and other States, the welcome news of Republican triumph. You will hear such a return from us as will make you happy. [Applause.]

Fellow-soldiers, I have said more than I intended to say. [Cries of "Go on."] My fellow-soldiers, I would have gone on merely to interest you a few hours longer [laughter], but I find there is one here that you much more desire to hear than you do me—a greater man and a better man, and one that you and I are working for. As soon as the report on Permanent Organization is read, you will have the pleasure of hearing the great statesman from the State of Massachusetts. I thank you for the compliment you have bestowed upon me. [Applause.]

On the conclusion of General Logan's remarks, Senator Wilson was loudly called for. The Senator was received with cheer upon cheer, the whole audience rising to their feet. Gen. Logan, in introducing him, said: "I have the honor of introducing to you that distinguished Christian statesman, the Hon. Henry Wilson, of Massachusetts, the next Vice-President of the United States." Senator Wilson spoke as follows:—

SPEECH OF SENATOR WILSON.

Be assured, gentlemen, that I am glad to look into your faces to-day, and I am grateful to you for your generous welcome. I am glad to see this representative assemblage of brave men who saved my country on the battle-field. I know something of the origin of the great civil war. I know something of the self-sacrificing patriotism of the men who left homes, fathers, mothers, sisters, brothers, wives, and children, and bared their bosoms against the blows of the enemy of the country. I know that they were never inspired by hate, but by love of country and love of liberty; and history will record the grand fact that the great uprising of the country in the spring of 1861 was an uprising of patriots, and not an uprising for hate or for vengeance. You loved your country, and your whole country. You loved the people of the country, and the people of the whole country; and through those four years of blood you labored on—struggled in victory and defeat alike—inspired by lofty patriotism, and never guided by vengeance; and to-day we meet here to do something more to perpetuate what you won on the battle-field, and that, too, for your country, and for the aggrandizement of no set of men on earth. Gentlemen, it was my privilege during those four years of bloody strife to act as Chairman of the Military Committee of the Senate of the United States, and I am proud to say to-day that in all the legislation of Congress, in all the confirmations of the many thousands that came before us, we always endeavored to do justice to the brave men who were fighting for the country, and we never asked the question what their political sentiments were. I know something of the self-sacrificing men that went to the field, fought, bled, and many of them died to save the country; and, gentlemen, while I would perpetuate no feeling of hate—while I would be generous, magnanimous and loving to all portions of my country, God willing, I would never forget the self-sacrificing patriotism, heroic valor, and consecrated devotion of the men who fought to save the country. [Applause]. I would build monuments all over the land for those who died for their country. [Applause.] I would keep the battles on the sacred flags that were laid away. I would, if I had the power, write the grand deeds of the defenders of the Union in letters of living light on the broad arches of the skies, so that all men, as they look heavenward, might be inspired by their noble example. [Applause.] You come here to-day, gentlemen, to encourage your countrymen who are striving to carry out in the action of the country what you fought to establish. May God prosper and bless you in these efforts, and I am sure your words, your example and your courage will inspire our countrymen, and we shall win a glorious victory for the cause of the great party to which we belong and which we believe to be the party of patriotism and the party of liberty in America. [Loud applause.] Gentlemen, in the dark and troubled night of war, when you were struggling in front of rebel legions, when our hospitals were filled with sick, wounded, and dying men, we could take your cause and our cause into our closets, and, on our bended knees, invoke God's blessing upon you. Hundreds of thousands of your countrymen did it—noble men and noble women did it; and to-day, gentlemen, we are fighting for the same cause; and the same ideas are on our banners to-day, and we can ask the support of the good men of our own country, the sympathies of loving men the wide world over, and the blessing of Almighty God upon our labor. Gentlemen, I will detain you no longer. I thank you a thousand times for this great assemblage here, and I thank you for your kind reception. God bless you all! [Applause.]

THE PERMANENT OFFICERS.

General Allen Rutherford, on behalf of the Committee on Permanent Organization, then submitted the following list of the Vice-Presidents and Secretaries chosen to represent the several States and Territories:—

Massachusetts—Vice-Presidents, James H. Barnes and Col. C. G. Attwood; Secretaries, Gen. Joseph F. Pickett, Capt. G. S. Merrill.

Ohio Vice-Presidents, Gen. G. M. Barber and Gen. P. S. Slevin; Secretaries, Col. W. F. Hinman and Capt. M. Blanchard.

New Jersey—Vice-Presidents, Col. Wm. Ward and Col. J. Madison Drake; Secretaries, Maj. J. B. Brose, L. C. Rice.

Wisconsin—Gen. L. Fairchild, Sergeant P. Stackhouse; Secretaries, Maj. W. H. Plunkett, Capt. E. M. Truell.

Georgia—Capt. C. H. Townsend, Capt. A. B. Clark; Secretaries, Sergeant George H. Stone, Sergeant W. H. Thomas.

Michigan—Maj. S. E. Graves, Gen. W. A. Throop; Secretaries, A. M. Edwards, Gen. F. L. Swift.

New Hampshire—Gen. S. G. Griffin, Gen. W. Harriman; Secretaries, Gen. H. B. Titus, Maj. Ed. Vaughan.

Rhode Island—Vice-Presidents, Gen. Nathan Goff, Capt. T. F. Usher; Secretaries, Surgeon Howard King, Sergeant R. F. Nicoli.

Connecticut—Col. C. L. Upham, Gen. H. W. Wessells; Secretaries, Adjt. C. A. Jewell, Maj. S. J. Corey.

New York—Gen. James Jourdan, Gen. W. S. Hillyer; Secretaries, Sergt.-Maj. S. Williams, Col. A. P. Ketchum.

Pennsylvania—Gen. J. T. Owens, Gen. J. B. Sweitzer; Secretaries, Col. A. M. Jones, Gen. H. H. Bingham.

Illinois—Gen. J. C. Smith, Col. Owen Stewart; Secretaries, Capt. T. E. Lonergan and Capt. T. E. Sherman.

Delaware—Lieut. James Lewis, Lieut. A. Vandever; Secretaries, Capt. E. C. Shortzenberg and James H. A. Myers.

Maryland—Maj. Geo. T. Cassell, Col. H. Adreon; Secretaries, J. R. King and Capt. R. Gross.

Iowa—Gen. E. W. Rice, Col. G. A. Stewart; Secretaries, Col. R. M. Littler and Capt. J. McElroy.

Virginia—Maj. E. E. White, Capt. W. A. McNulty; Secretaries, Capt. B. C. Cook and William J. Johnston.

West Virginia—Gen. B. F. Kelley, Gen. T. M. Harris; Secretaries, Maj. M. B. C. Wright and Capt. B. B. Dovener.

North Carolina—Gen. Allen Rutherford, Sergeant G. D. Watson; Secretaries, Maj. J. W. Schenk and Capt. E. M. Shoemaker.

Texas—Gen. W. T. Clark and Gen. James Davidson; Secretaries, Capt. J. E. Whittlesey and Capt. T. Finn.

Minnesota—Gen. J. H. Baker, C. A. Drew.

Tennessee—Col. W. F. Prosser, Col. B. Lewis; Secretaries, Capt. A. J. Ricks, Col. D. W. Glassie.

Kentucky—Gen. A. P. Hall, Gen. S. W. Price; Secretaries, Gen. C. P. Wilcox, Capt. J. D. Eaton.

Missouri—Col. J. B. Jones, Capt. G. W. Cooper; Secretaries, Col. J. A. Joyce, Capt. R. E. Brien.

Louisiana—Col. Chas. W. Lowell, Lieut. W. H. Webster; Secretaries, Capt. F. Morley, Lieut. Oscar A. Rice.

Mississippi—Capt. J. C. Tucker, Col. A. Warner; Secretaries, Capt. C. W. Clark, Maj. O. C. French.

Florida—Gen. H. Jenkins, Capt. A. A. Kuight; Secretaries, Capt. E. M. Cheney, Capt. D. Eagan.

Colorado—Col. J. M. Hall, Gen. D. L. Smith; Secretaries, Col. J. D. Wells and E. W. Stanton.

Montana—Gen. W. F. Scribner, Gen John C. Blane.

California—Lieut. W. H. Lowrie, Capt. Hartmier; Secretaries, J. Mason Kline, Col. Robert M. Lee.

District of Columbia—Col. Hermann Seligson and A. A. Shisslar; Secretaries, Geo. J. Bond, J. W. Jordan, U. S. Navy.

Utah—Gen. G. B. Maxwell, Col. Wm. M. Johns; Secretaries, Capt. T. H. Bates, E. B. Zabriskie and Maj. A. K. Smith.

South Carolina—Vice-Presidents, Capt. J. L. Little, Lieut. Chas. Sammis; Secretaries, Gen. Wm. Gurney, Maj. T. D. Corbin.

Alabama—Vice-Presidents, Gen. R. N. Healy, Gen. Geo. H. Patrick; Secretaries, Col. C. Cadle, Col. T. Kinsman.

General James A. Garfield, appearing upon the stage, was loudly called for, and, being introduced by the Chairman, spoke as follows:—

SPEECH OF GENERAL GARFIELD.

FELLOW-SOLDIERS—I know I shall speak the sentiments of every man in this audience when I say that whatever pride we have in the past, whatever pride we brought back from the battle-fields, we joyfully laid that pride and glory upon one altar, and are all glad to merge the title of soldiers in a greater one—that of American citizen. We recognize that as the highest title. Fighting or laboring, living or dying, it is as citizens of the Republic; American citizenship is the unit, which, being repeated by the number of our population, makes the nation and its glory. American citizenship is the grand level from which all our heights and depths of political life are measured. For my part, I preferred that this should be our only measure of political questions. It was my hope when the war ended that we might meet only socially, to renew the friendships and memories of the past, and that no word of political discord should be heard in a soldier-gathering. But now, for the first time, our right to mingle in the political contests of the day is challenged, if not denied. We are here to answer that challenge. We are told that the time of the soldier in politics is past, because his presence reminds some of our fellow-citizens of defeat. We are here to respond to this impertinent assumption. We never asked the twenty-two rebel officers to retire who to-day hold seats in the American Congress. They are there in their higher rights of American citizenship, and no man says them nay for sitting in their places; and shall the fifty Union soldiers who are sitting in the Senate and House, retire because they were soldiers? [Cries of "No! no!"] A great Senator said, and published it to the people, that a soldier in the Executive Chair is a menace. He says our victories over rebellion "should not be inscribed on regimental colors," and that the presence in the Executive Chair of our leader in the late war is "a regimental color with a forbidden inscription," and should be kept there no longer. We are here to-day to say that if General Grant is a banner—he is our banner—the banner of the Republic—inscribed with the record of our great national victories. They ask us to haul down that color, to strike our banner. That banner we will not strike. [Cries of "Never! never!"] They may apply to General Grant all the tests and criticisms of political life; but, when they strike him because he was a soldier, we will rally round him again and repel the ignoble and unpatriotic assault. They say he must be put aside, as an obstacle to reconciliation and peace with the South. I repel this as a wicked slander, against not only General Grant, but against all who fought under his leadership. It is because of these assaults, that here to-day, for the first time in my life, I invoke the soldier-associations into the political contest. There is not a grave in which a soldier sleeps in all this redeemed land but will be desecrated by this great slander. There is not a monument that points to God anywhere on the soil of the Republic that ought not to be demolished and ground to the earth, if for such a reason it is time for the soldier to retire. There is not a banner upon which your victories are inscribed, that ought not to be burned if the time has come for the soldier to retire. Thank God, the old banners are here! [Great applause.] The voice of battle is in you. [Applause.] And in your name I answer the slander of our defamers, that more noble, magnanimous, and gentle-hearted men never lived than the men who fought, bled, and died in defense of the Union during our late war. In the war there were four classes of men. The first were our comrades who shared with us the perils and glory of battle. We shall love those living and sacredly cherish the memories of those who are dead. Another class were our gallant foes. We fought and conquered them, and then treated them with the honors of war. There were two other classes; the deserter from our banner—we shot him; the spy from the enemy's camp—we hanged him. The same classes appear in the pending political struggle. I do not say that our political enemies to-day are all deserters and spies; but I do say that in the mixed political army that to-day confronts us, and which has the hardihood to call itself the party of reform, are found all the deserters from our camp, and all the scouts and intriguers of our old political enemies. Against these deserters and spies we throw the weight of our whole line. [Applause.] I did not come here to speak to you to-day. [Cries of "Go on!"] I came to welcome you, and to join you in declaring once more, that we are here to maintain the great principles for which we fought. Remember that after the battle of armies comes the battle of history. Whose ideas shall prevail in that new conflict? Our war was a mistake, a fearful failure, if we do not also conquer there. Until the ideas for which we contended are crystallized into the enduring forms of national life, we are not ready to ret've. We are not ready to retire until the great principles for which we fought are lifted up into the serene firmament of our national heaven, there to blaze for ever and ever. [Applause.]

SPEECH OF GENERAL S. G. GRIFFIN.

General S. G. Griffin, of New Hampshire, being called for, came forward and said:—

Mr. President and Comrades—I thank you for the honor you have conferred upon me, and for the opportunity thus offered me to say a word in favor of the cause which has brought us here to-day.

A great contest is impending, differing, it is true, from that which led us to the field in 1861, but scarcely less important than that. We are in a great presidential contest, and the battle-ground of that contest is to be here in Pennsylvania. Elect our gallant comrade, John F. Hartranft, Governor of this State, and the election of General Grant is assured. Elect Hartranft, and we will give Grant five thousand majority in New Hampshire, and we will carry Connecticut, Indiana, and New York in November.

Defeat Hartranft, and every one of those States is left in doubt, as will also be the election of General Grant. We have rallied here from New Hampshire, from Maine, from Wisconsin, from Dakota, from California, from every one of the thirty-seven States in behalf of the cause of the Union, and of right government, as we did in 1861.

The great question for us to decide is whether we shall continue in power that party which has been on the right side of every question every time and all the time for the last fifteen years, and which, by the wisdom of its policy and measures, in spite of the incubus of an enormous debt and all the drawbacks incident to a great civil war so recently waged, has given the country a prosperity that is unparalleled in the history of nations, or whether we will abandon that party and put in its place a party that has been on the wrong side of every question every time and all the time for the last ten or fifteen years, and which has opposed every one of those great and beneficent measures which have brought the nation up to the proud position it occupies to-day.

Whether we will stand by that party which carried the Republic so gloriously through a gigantic rebellion, and has given it a career of honor and success and renown among the nations of the earth, and that is still bearing it onward on the grand platform of "freedom for all men" and the "rights of citizenship for all men," or whether we will turn our backs upon that party and put in its place one whose leaders inaugurated and carried on that rebellion, and attempted to destroy this republic—a party whose great and leading principle has been the support, the extension, and the perpetuation of human slavery—a party which has acted as the champion of slave in opposition to free labor; whether we will continue in power that party which has made for itself the most glorious record ever made by any party in any nation under heaven, and that is still marching on in that same grandly progressive course, or whether we will repudiate that party, and place in power a party which has been compelled to abandon every one of its principles, every one of its positions, every one of its measures, and come over and adopt our principles, our platform, and even to enlist the disappointed aspirants for place in our party, and adopt them as their leaders. Whether we will stand by that party which has made for itself a financial record that challenges the admiration of the world, that has reduced taxation, that has paid one-eighth of our whole national war-debt within the last three years, and at the same time has given the country its present wonderful prosperity, or whether we will place in power that party which is pledged to pay pensions and bounties to rebel soldiers, pay for the emancipated slaves, pay the claims of rebels for property destroyed during the war, and pay the rebel war-debt.

My comrades, we remember at the close of the war in 1865, how earnest and how universal was the expression of gratitude to the soldiers for the services they had performed; how frequently we heard the expression that there was "one debt which this nation never could repay, and that was the debt of gratitude it owed the soldiers who had preserved the Union." That was at that time the honest expression of the opinions and feelings of the patriotic people of the country.

Has the nation so soon forgotten that debt of gratitude? Are we about to turn our backs upon that man who, when the nation was plunged into a civil war, volunteered his services and pledged his life to the Government; and, when leader after leader had attempted the command of our armies and failed, and all looked dark and discouraging, and the army and the people were disheartened and demoralized, rose up from obscurity step by step by his own merits, without political influence, until he was placed in command of all the armies of these United States, and by his powerful intellect, his military genius, and his giant grasp, crushed out the rebellion and conquered a peace, and inaugurated the proudest career for the country ever recorded in history? [Cheers.] Shall we turn our backs upon that man and put in his place Horace Greeley, whose nomination by the Cincinnati Convention was received with derisive laughter by the whole nation, who, of all the prominent men of this country is the most unstable, the least to be relied upon; who is one thing to-day, another thing to-morrow; who is, perhaps, the most prolific writer in this country in favor of protection, and yet accepts the nomination of a free-trade party; who, by his insane cry of "On to Richmond," heralded through the country by the New York *Tribune*, is responsible more than any other man for the disaster of Bull Run; and yet, when General Grant had hammered the rebellion out until it was so thin everybody else could see through it, and knew that one grip more would crush it like the merest shell, trembled with fear like an arrant coward, and was for giving up everything, acknowledging ourselves beaten, and submitting, like whipped curs, to the dictation of the people whom we had conquered?

Are we going to allow one of the noblest, one of the purest, one of the most successful public servants we ever had to be ignominiously defeated? [Cries of "Never."] That man who conquered and put down the rebellion, who did more than any other man to liberate the freedmen and restore to them their inherent and God-given rights, and who gave us the proud history of Donelson, and Vicksburg, and Petersburg, and Appomattox—are we going to allow him to be defeated by Horace Greeley, that man who has sold himself for a mess of potage, who has bartered his soul and all his life-long principles for the nomination to the presidency by the Democratic party? Who are the friends of Greeley? The old rebel element at the South, the opponents of the war at the North, Tammany democrats who are desperately anxious to get their hands into the Treasury, soreheads, and disappointed office-seekers.

And who are the friends of Grant? The business men of this nation, who desire its financial success and prosperity, the loyal and patriotic element throughout the land, those noble men and women who, by their labors, their prayers, and their donations, gave such powerful moral encouragement to the Government during the dark days of the war, and those brave men who tendered their lives to the Republic and won its victories on sea and land.

We unfurl our national flag and place thereon, in these presidential contests, the names of Grant and Wilson. How just and appropriate that we place there, as our candidate, the name of him who carried that flag so triumphantly through so many glorious campaigns and through so many hard-fought battles, and who, with his sword, has won for it a respect and surrounded it with a halo of glory such as had never been seen before. But what lover of his country would not blush with shame and indignation to see upon that flag, as a presidential candidate, the name of Jefferson Davis? But, gentlemen, when you see upon that flag the name of Horace Greeley, you may just as well read it Jefferson Davis, for it means precisely the same thing.

In response to loud calls, General Stewart L. Woodford, of New York, ascended the platform and spoke as follows:—

SPEECH OF GENERAL WOODFORD.

MR. CHAIRMAN AND COMRADES—You were citizens before you became soldiers. You volunteered at the call of an imperi-led nation, that you might fulfill the highest duty of citizenship—the duty of offering life in defense of fatherland. When the rebellion had been suppressed—you were mustered out and resumed the old avocations of peaceful industry. You were and are citizens still. You assert no claim to special recognition and honor among your fellows because of your army service. You recognize that you only sought to do your duty. You do not admit that, because you were soldiers when the nation needed men ready to dare, to do, to die, you are, therefore, in these happy days of peace to be denied your equal share in the councils of the Government, your equal participation in all the privileges as well as in all the responsibilities of citizenship.

You do not gather here to-day in these many thousands to claim any right as soldiers to rule the land which as soldiers you saved. But you come as citizens, who, because of your sacrifice and service, believe that you value this government aright, to do what you properly can to keep the National Administration in wise, patriotic, and honest hands.

While you come with no boast of the past, you also come with no apology for your gathering. You feel that your comradeship in battle justifies your taking counsel of each other as to your duties in peace.

We have met to say frankly and directly to our comrades, and all the people, that we are still grateful to the Republican party for all its grand record and work.

It always, alike in victory and defeat, believed in the cause for which we fought. When battle and disease thinned our ranks, it always sought to send fresh men to the front. When the Democratic party, in that sad summer of 1864, gathered in convention, pronounced the prosecution of the war a failure, and counseled surrender, the Republican party pledged the Government to draft the last man and expend the last dollar in crushing rebellion and maintaining the national unity. With grand amen the nation responded to such pledge and appeal. Kneeling among the graves of our fallen soldiers, the people renewed the vow of Sumter. In that faith we conquered. Aye, we are grateful to the Republican party for its trust and resolution, for the sincere honors which it always paid to our fallen, for its earnest effort to care for our disabled comrades living, and the widows and orphans of our comrades dead.

But, while we thus come with gratitude to the Republican party, we come with no spirit of hate toward our late antagonists in battle. We revive no memory of bitterness. We pluck no embers of strife from out the ashes of the past.

We respect the sincerity of the men who were our foes in open conflict, but who are now our fellows in citizenship and in the duty of a common loyalty to a common country, as only those can respect them who tested their endurance and valor on many fields.

We have even forgiven them for Andersonville and Libby, for we believed that the horrors of these prison-pens sprang from the terrible teachings and influences of slavery. We charged the crime upon slavery, and have never kept those agonies as subjects of revengeful memory against the men of the South and soldiers of the rebellion. We destroyed slavery, and then forgave Andersonville.

We should never have thus ourselves referred to the merciful and generous record of the Union Army, had not the constant attacks and misrepresentations of a partisan press rendered some brief words timely and just. Let history, not mere profession, bear witness.

Lee surrendered his army. The terms of that surrender were as generous and humane as any recorded in the annals of civilized warfare. Grant allowed each officer to keep his

4

sword, that none might feel personal dishonor. Each man was permitted to retain his horse, that he might return to his home, plow his fields, and make crops for the support of his family. Supplies were issued to the beaten foe. You are silently recalling how, as by instinct, you opened your haversacks on the Sabbath morn of that surrender, and shared your scanty rations with the men whom you had fought for four long, bloody years. You recall how, when Andrew Johnson, in the first frenzy of his passion, sought to break the terms of Grant's parole, to arrest Lee and place him on trial, our chieftain replied that, so long as the Confederate soldiers obeyed the law and kept the peace, the parole at Appomattox should protect them, and tendered his resignation as General if good faith was to be violated.

The war being ended we sought peace. We prayed for reconciliation. We reached out hands of hearty fellowship to all who would accept such fellowship on the basis of sincere submission to the law and unconditional loyalty. From that hour until now, we have never counseled or consented to any injustice or revenge towards the South. We forgave our foe. Good faith and simple manhood required us to secure an absolute protection to all who had been our friends and allies at the South during the struggle. Good faith and simple manhood required us to give this protection ourselves, if the men of the South did not grant it themselves.

This is the whole spirit of the Constitutional amendments. Mercy could grant no more than absolute forgiveness to our foe. Honor could consent to no less than absolute protection to the loyal white and the enfranchised black.

We desire entire and permanent reconciliation to-day. In war we fought to preserve our national unity, and thus to obtain enduring peace. In peace we heartily strive to secure complete reconciliation. That reconciliation will be most thorough and lasting which shall be based upon impartial laws impartially enforced. Thus it will be strengthened by justice as well as love.

When none shall seek to coerce the votes of the lowly; when education shall be afforded to all the children of the land, black as well as white; when the true dignity of labor shall be recognized; when, in a word, not merely the letter, but the practical administration of the law shall secure the personal and political rights of all our citizens, throughout all the States, reconciliation will be complete. For these ends let us patiently labor, in the sure faith, that we labor not in vain. We have met to say frankly and directly to our comrades, and to all the people, that we believe that the continued ascendency of the Republican party, in the council-halls of the nation, and in the administration of the Government, is still essential to the full security of the results of the war; still essential to the protection of the loyal whites and the enfranchised blacks of the South; still essential to the certain payment of their justly deserved pensions to our disabled living comrades and to the widows and orphans of our dead; still essential to the maintenance of our financial credit and our financial welfare; still essential to the true being of the laboring classes and to the sure maintenance of that honorable peace with all nations, so necessary to repair the losses of war, to develop our great and varied material resources, and to solidify that development into permanent prosperity.

We have met to say frankly and directly to our commands and to all the people, that we thoroughly believe in Ulysses S. Grant as President, just as we believe in him as soldier. That as we knew him to be brave in battle, we now know him to be faithful in peace. That as we then knew him to be wise in plan, skillful in strategy, and sure in execution, we now know him to be practical in statesmanship, merciful in policy, honest in administration, and inflexible in the enforcement of the law. [Loud and prolonged applause.]

One unbroken line of victories, from Belmont to Appomattox, the crushed rebellion, and the surrendered Confederacy, placed his name forever among the few great captains of history, and justified all our faith in Ulysses S. Grant as a soldier.

The steady collection of the revenue; the steady reduction of taxation; the steady diminution of the national debt; the steady decline in the price of gold; the steady increase in the value of our paper currency and of our national bonds; the steady enforcement of the laws; the repression of the Ku-Klux disorders, and the steady growth of confidence, and of a substantial prosperity throughout the South; the earnest and humane attempt to deal kindly and justly with the Indian tribes; the manly submission of personal judgment and will to the judgment and will of the people, so grandly shown in his cheerful surrender of the San Domingo scheme; the resolute and heroic purpose to place before the nations an example of settling their quarrels by peaceful arbitration rather than by the sword, so faithfully carried out in the Alabama negotiations, and now so happily crowned with success among the hills of Switzerland: all these form an unbroken line of peaceful victories, which place the name of Ulysses S. Grant forever among the few great statesmen of the age, which justify the love of his old comrades, and deserve the gratitude of the nation.

Such, in direct words, are the reasons why we have gathered from almost every State in the land. May the old spirit of hearty comradeship, which bound us so closely together in other days, still be and abide with us.

As we take each others' hands and look in each others' faces, old memories come back—memories of the living and the dead. With these let us recall the high resolve, the pure purpose, which consecrated our enlistment. Let us also recall the generous forgiveness and hearty fraternity which filled all hearts when the strife was ended.

Thus shall we take counsel together as patriots rather than partisans. Thus shall we seek success, not for self or section, but for the good of all our common country and the highest welfare of all our fellow-citizens.

Gov. Edward F. Noyes, of Ohio, was loudly called. On coming forward he said :—

ADDRESS OF GOVERNOR NOYES.

FELLOW-SOLDIERS—We are under contract to leave this building to-night at five o'clock, and I find it is five minutes past five now. Comrades, we are here to express together our continued confidence in the integrity, in the capacity, and in the patriotism of our great captain. We have come here to enter our solemn protest against the slanders which have been heaped upon his name. We are here also to express our confidence in that grand old party which supported the soldiers while they were fighting the battles of the nation. Once more, my friends, as we remember the four years of our bloody war; the half-million of our comrades who sleep the sleep that knows no waking; as we remember the half-million of cripples that go up and down the land suffering all the twinges of pain that weather-changes bring soldiers; when we remember how the black crape was hung on your doors; as we remember how you were called upon to leave your homes and make great sacrifices for us while you were fighting for our country, we are not disposed to forget him who led us to victory when all others had failed, and saved an imperiled country. We have met to get inspiration from each other. We go as missionaries among the people, to call to their minds the great deeds of our leader. We rely upon the justice of our cause. We have faith in that God who protected us during the stormy years of war. We go forth in faith that we shall be successful. May God prosper the right! [Applause.]

The hour for adjournment having passed, General Logan announced that the Convention would reassemble promptly at 10 o'clock next day—Wednesday—and that the first business in order would be the reception of the Report of the Committee on Resolutions. The proceedings of the day were concluded by singing the long-measure doxology, "Praise God from whom all blessings flow," to the tune of "Old Hundred," the audience, all standing, joining in the singing of this grand and impressive benediction.

SECOND DAY'S PROCEEDINGS.

WEDNESDAY, SEPTEMBER 18, 1872.

At 10 o'clock, Chairman Logan called the convention to order. Rev. John S. Sands, of Pittsburg, offered the following prayer:—

OPENING PRAYER.

O, Thou great God of all nations, Thou great God of this nation, we come before Thee this morning, invoking Thy presence and Thy blessing. We thank Thee for this country of ours, with its broad acres, with its teeming population, with its good and wise government; we thank Thee, O God, for its brave defenders, who, in the hour of their country's danger, were filled with a spirit of patriotism, and who went forth against their enemies and imperilled their lives in its defense; we thank Thee that Thou hast permitted so many of them to meet together on this occasion; we thank Thee that Thou hast blessed them in their deliberations during the former sessions of this Convention, and we pray Thee that Thou wilt bless them this morning and through this day.

We thank Thee, O God, for all Thy blessings; we thank Thee for the peace, order, and quiet of our city. Help us while we do honor to those who in their country's hour of danger fought for their country's flag; and, while we drop a tear in remembrance of those who laid their lives down for their country's salvation and defense, oh, help us to remember that great sacrifice once made in which the Son of God himself laid down his life for us all.

Bless, O God, the officers of this convention; bless the soldiers and sailors here assembled; bless the President of the United States and all his advisers; and bless all our citizens. God of our refuge and our strength, lift us higher and higher as a nation, till Thy glory shines upon us. Grant us our prayer for Jesus' sake. Amen.

In the interval which followed the prayer, Nevin & Dean's band, from Chicago, played a medley which was loudly applauded, and the Welsh Glee Club, of Pittsburg, sang several songs with fine effect. The Marine Band, of Washington City, played several selections from operas, by request. The Committee on Resolutions not being ready to report, the band of the Forty-seventh New York Regiment played "Our Nation's Song," which was loudly applauded.

General Joseph C. Abbott, of North Carolina, from the Committee of Resolutions, said:—

REMARKS OF GENERAL ABBOTT.

The Committee on Resolutions have instructed me to present the resolutions which I hold in my hand, as a declaration of principles to be submitted to the Convention. I will ask the Secretary of the Convention to read them.

The resolutions were read by the Secretary, and are as follows:—

RESOLUTIONS OF THE CONVENTION.

We, the soldiers and sailors who served in the Union Army and Navy during the late war, in mass convention in Pittsburg assembled, for the purpose of expressing our firm convictions upon issues which are logical results of the war, do affirm:—

1. That it is a source of unmingled pleasure to meet again, and, reviving the memories of our campaign for union and liberty, thence to draw lessons for present duty and future guidance.

2. We reaffirm our devotion to the union of the States; the arbitrament of war has decreed that we are one nation, with one flag, with liberty and equality before the law for all men; and national authority is essential to establish, protect, and defend liberty and the inalienable rights of the people.

3. We enter our solemn protest against transferring the control of the Army and Navy, the Treasury and the entire Government, and the Constitutional Amendments, with the execution of the laws themselves, to an unholy and corrupt coalition composed chiefly of elements but recently in open hostility to them all.

4. We cherish no spirit of revenge toward our fellow-citizens of the South; the magnanimity of our late Commander-in-Chief on the field of Appomattox was a sufficient pledge of the Union Army that the "bloody chasm" of the war was closed; and "with malice toward none, but with charity for all," we extend the right hand of fellowship to all those who accept, in good faith, the results of the war, and who will extend to every American citizen, of whatever race or color, the rights which are solemnly guaranteed by the Constitution of the United States and the laws made in pursuance thereof.

5. Reposing implicit confidence in the patriotism and gratitude of the nation, we confide to it every interest of the Union soldier; and we here express our most cordial appreciation of the unparalleled generosity of the people, as expressed through Congress in the laws providing pensions and bounties, and we fully believe that any inequalities which may appear will be cheerfully and promptly corrected.

6. We gladly and proudly reaffirm our enthusiastic confidence in the integrity, patriotism, and ability of President Grant. We point to his messages for opinions and recommendations in harmony with the most advanced political sentiments. We point to the condition of the country in all its relations, foreign and domestic, for the proof that its laws are well administered and its honor maintained. We rejoice to see associated with him the incorruptible and indefatigable patriot and representative man of American institutions, Henry Wilson, of Massachusetts

7. We pledge our steady and earnest support to President Grant and Congress in reforming the civil service and establishing the highest standard of honor and fidelity among all the servants of the Government.

8. Although this Convention is purely national in its inception and purposes, we cannot refrain from expressing our sympathy and giving our cordial support to our gallant comrade leading the column in Pennsylvania, whose illustrious record as a brave and faithful soldier should endear him to every loyal heart.

THANKS OF THE CONVENTION TO PITTSBURG.

General Burnside said :—

Lest we might separate in haste, I rise to make the motion that we, as soldiers and sailors, thank the loyal and good people of Pittsburg for their kind treatment to us during our stay in their city, and that the thanks of this Convention be given to the Veterans' Resident Committee, who have in reality done all the work of giving us the grand reception which we have received.

The motion of General Burnside was adopted, the Convention rising *en masse* and cheering in response to his suggestion. A motion was then made for the Convention to adjourn *sine die.* Pending the adoption of this motion, General Logan, the Chairman, said :—

* REMARKS OF GENERAL LOGAN.

COMRADES—One word before we return to our homes. When our enemies tell us to be reconciled to those who fought against the Government, let us tell them that there is no reconciliation required on our part. We are reconciled to our country, to its honor and glory, to its Constitution, and to the old banner of our fathers; and when those men who draw their blades against this Government become themselves reconciled to the old banner, we will be reconciled to them. [Applause.] It is on their part, and not on ours. Let us go to our homes in cities, towns, hamlets, and villages, determined to carry the fruits of our great victories with us. Let not these, like Dead Sea fruit, be turned to ashes on our lips. Let each man, when he goes to his home, insist on all his friends voting the whole Republican ticket. A grand Republican triumph is what we want, and what we must have, to secure peace, happiness, and prosperity in this land. [Applause.]

At the suggestion of General Hawley, three rousing cheers were given for Grant and Wilson, after which the members of the Convention separated, most of them to attend the grand mass meeting at Friendship Grove, where General B. F. Butler, of Massachusetts, delivered one of the best speeches of the campaign. To the disappointment of the National Committee no report of this speech was taken ; and so synopsis can do adequate justice to his masterly effort on this occasion. Probably no audience so large has been assembled during this campaign, and a lasting impression was made upon the thousands gathered there by his unanswerable arguments.

VETERANS' NATIONAL COMMITTEE.

The following are the names of the Veterans' National Committee, appointed by the Convention :—

Gen. A. E. Burnside, Chairman.
Gen. Joseph R. Hawley, Vice-Chairman.
Col. L. E. Dudley, Secretary.
Arkansas—Gen. Powell Clayton.
Alabama—Major R. M. Reynolds.
California—Col. W. E. McArthur.
Connecticut—Gen. J. R. Hawley.
Delaware—Lieut. John M. Dunn.
Florida—Gen. Charles M. Hamilton.
Georgia—Sergt. William H. Thomas.
Indiana—Gen. Nathan Kimball.
Illinois—Gen. Julius White.
Iowa—Capt. J. R. Hammond.

Kansas—Major J. C. Wilkinshaw.
Kentucky—Capt. P. S. Reeves.
Louisiana—Lieut. W. H. Webster.
Maine—Gen. Selden Conner.
Massachusetts—Gen. Horace Binney Sargent.
Michigan—Major E. B. Wright.
Minnesota—Gen. J. H. Baker.
Missouri—Gen. John S. Cavender.
Mississippi—Capt. H. R. Pease.
Maryland—Major W. L. Vanderlip.
New Hampshire—Gen. S. G. Griffin.
New York—Col. L. E. Dudley.
Nevada—No one named.

New Jersey—Col. F. H. Harris.
Nebraska—Gen. John M. Thayer.
North Carolina—Gen. Allen Rutherford.
Ohio—Gen. James B. Barnett.
Oregon—No one named.
Pennsylvania—Gen. A. L. Pearson.
Rhode Island—Gen. Chas. R. Brayton.
South Carolina—
Tennessee—Gen. R. F. Patterson.
Texas—Major Thomas Smith.
Vermont—

Virginia—Col. S. E. Chamberlain.
West Virginia—Capt. John Carlin.
Wisconsin—Col. Thomas Reynolds.
Arizona—Col. Drake De Kay.
Colorado—Gen. Ed. S. McCook.
Dakota—Gen. Edwin McCook.
Montana—Col. L. B. Church.
New Mexico—Col. William Breeden.
Washington—
District of Columbia—Gen. N. P. Chipman.
At Large—Gen. A. E. Burnside.

EXECUTIVE COMMITTEE.

At a meeting of the Committee, held at Pittsburg, the chairman was directed to announce an Executive Committee, of which the officers of the General Committee should be *ex-officio* members and officers. In accordance with that resolution, the chairman has announced the following named veterans as said committee:—

Gen. Horace Binney Sargent, Massachusetts.
Gen. J. H. Baker, Minnesota.
Col. F. H. Harris, New Jersey.

Gen. Allen Rutherford, North Carolina.
Col. Drake De Kay, Arizona.

www.ingramcontent.com/pod-product-compliance
Lightning Source LLC
Chambersburg PA
CBHW032140270626
47172CB00009B/729